RESURRECTING
MARX

The Analytical Marxism ...

Fr ... ice

0887388787

SOCIAL
PHILOSOPHY
& POLICY CENTER

RESURRECTING
MARX

The Analytical Marxists on
Freedom, Exploitation, and Justice

David Gordon

transaction

Transaction Books
New Brunswick (USA) and London (UK)

Published by the Social Philosophy and Policy Center and by Transaction Publishers 1990.

Library of Congress Cataloging-in-Publication Data.

Gordon, David, 1948–
    Resurrecting Marx : the analytical Marxists on exploitation, freedom, and justice / by David Gordon.
        p.   cm. — (Studies in social philosphy and policy : no. 14)
    Includes index.
    ISBN 0-88738-390-4. — ISBN 0-88738-878-7 (pbk.)
    1. Socialism.   2. Marx, Karl, 1818–1883. Kapital.   3. Labor theory of value.   4. Liberty.   I. Title.   II. Series: Studies in social philosophy & policy ; no. 14.
    HX73.G66   1990
    335.4′1—dc20   90-41619
                                                                          CIP

Cover Design: Kent Lytle

In memory of my dear friend and teacher,
Walter F. Starkie

Series Editor: Ellen Frankel Paul
Series Managing Editor: Dan Greenberg

The Social Philosophy and Policy Center, founded in 1981, is an interdisciplinary research institution whose principal mission is the examination of public policy issues from a philosophical perspective. In pursuit of this objective, the Center supports the work of scholars in the fields of political science, philosophy, law, and economics. In addition to the book series, the Center hosts scholarly conferences and edits an interdisciplinary professional journal, *Social Philosophy & Policy*. For further information on the Center, write to the: Social Philosophy and Policy Center, Bowling Green State University, Bowling Green, OH 43403.

Contents

Acknowledgments

I should first of all like to thank the Social Philosophy and Policy Center of Bowling Green State University and the Earhart Foundation for sponsoring my work. Professor Ellen Frankel Paul of the Center has been an ideal editor, offering both penetrating comments and encouragement. By refusing to accept my habitual procrastination, she bears primary responsibility for the appearance of this book. Dan Greenberg, the Center's Managing Editor, materially improved the manuscript through careful copyediting.

In revising my book, I have been greatly aided by comments from Robert Nozick and from an anonymous reader. I have also benefited a great deal from many years of conversations with Nozick.

I have discussed some of the issues covered in the book with Murray Rothbard, James Sadowsky, S. J., John Gray, Jeremy Shearmur, Hans Hoppe, Ralph Raico, Ronald Hamowy, and George Resch. To all of them, my thanks.

My friend and typist, Bill Delaney, has endured my microscopic handwriting for more years than he deserves.

Most of all, I am grateful to my parents for their encouragement and support. None of the persons just mentioned assumes any responsibility for the contents of this book (unless, of course, any of them wants to).

Some readers, I hope, will approach the book with much more sympathy for Marxism than I have. I hope they will not be put off by the polemical tone I have sometimes adopted. Whatever one thinks of my tone or my political views—the nature of which, I fear, will soon become obvious—the arguments presented here stand or fall by themselves. Further, in spite of the criticisms I offer, I admire greatly the work of Jon Elster and G. A. Cohen.

Introduction

Marxism has enjoyed a revival in the American academy during the last fifteen years. In fields as diverse as literary criticism, history, law, and philosophy, new movements which take some aspects of Marxist thought as their inspiration have captivated scholars. This recrudescence of Marxism is somewhat surprising, since in the 1950s and 1960s mainstream economists had dismissed the elaborate system erected by Karl Marx in *Das Kapital* as a long-ago refuted relic.

Deconstructionists in English departments and Critical Legal Studies advocates in the law schools have been greatly influenced by aspects of Marxist thought, but what these movements lacked was a thoroughgoing reappraisal of the scientific basis of Marxism. Recently, philosophers and economists have stepped into this void, attempting to reevaluate Marx's fundamental concepts and, where necessary, reconstruct Marx from the ground up on a new, more rigorous basis.

These "analytical Marxists" contend that a Marxism purged of some of the outmoded views of its founders can withstand the criticisms that have led most mainstream social scientists to reject it. What guaranteed these new-style Marxists a ready audience was their adaptation of the techniques of modern philosophy and economics to Marxism. The members of the group—who include G. A. Cohen, Jon Elster, and John Roemer—believe that, far from being outmoded, the main doctrines of Marxism are still valid, albeit in radically refurbished form.

The work of the group has wider importance than as a contribution to the technicalities of Marxist economic theory. Their influence has been quite extensive, both within philosophy and the other humanities and social sciences that philosophical thought permeates. The analytical Marxists have launched a sophisticated attack on capitalism, charging that capitalist systems exploit labor. The arguments they have advanced on this topic

1

have exerted considerable influence on many outside the Marxist camp, for the question of whether capitalism is exploitative is vital to political philosophy. This question is the principal topic of this book. I agree with the group on the importance of analytic philosophy as a method for exploring questions in political philosophy. However, I shall argue that the analytical Marxists' critique of capitalism fails.

The book's initial chapter briefly describes the group and its principal tenets and methods. It introduces Cohen, Elster, and Roemer, the three principal figures of the group. Unlike Marx and Engels, these writers rest their case against capitalism on standard logic rather than dialectics.

One of the few uncontroversial remarks one can make about Marxism is that it is critical of capitalism. Chapter 2, "The Classical Marxist Assault on Capitalism," examines the basis of Marx's anti-capitalism. Marx argued that capitalists exploit the proletariat. This contention, in his opinion, was not an arbitrary value judgment, but an inevitable conclusion from the "law of motion" of capitalism—which he claimed to have discovered.

Marx's claim about exploitation, in my opinion, does not hold up to analysis. Marx's argument depends on his version of the labor theory of value, and it is radically flawed. Of necessity, some of the material in this chapter goes over familiar ground, yet a surprising conclusion will emerge: Marx's thesis of labor exploitation does not follow from the labor theory of value.

The analytical Marxists agree that the labor theory of value should be rejected. Their criticisms of the theory differ from those presented in Chapter 2, and are accordingly one of the topics discussed in a separate chapter: "The Analytical Marxist Rejection of Classical Marxism." This chapter emphasizes a central theme of the book: in their efforts to bring Marxism up to date, the analytical Marxists have criticized classical Marxism in withering terms.

If, as Chapter 3 shows, the analytical Marxists reject the labor theory of value, what happens to the claim that workers are exploited? John Roemer has offered the most detailed response to this query. He presents a new account of exploitation, based on the fact that people in a capitalist economy start out from unequal holdings of property. The chapter concludes with a rejection of Roemer's proposal. He has failed to make even a *prima facie* case that capitalism is exploitative.

The analytical school has not confined its efforts to the defense and reconstruction of Marxism. G. A. Cohen, whom I consider the most important adherent of the group, has argued strongly against the libertarian claim that individuals have a natural right to own private property. Cohen concentrates his fire on the most famous academic defense of libertarianism, Robert Nozick's *Anarchy, State, and Utopia* (1974). Cohen finds considerable force in the libertarian view that each person has ownership rights over his or her own body. He denies, however, that this right supports the right of individuals to own property.

In Chapter 4, "Analytical Marxism Versus Libertarian Rights," Cohen's arguments are rejected. He fastens too exclusively on details of Nozick's account, advancing criticisms of it that do not apply to other libertarian defenses of property rights. Cohen also assumes without justification that an analysis of property rights begins from the assumption of collective rights to use property.

Cohen has advanced another criticism of capitalism, one which has aroused considerable discussion. He maintains that the proletariat is "collectively unfree" under capitalism. Individual workers do not have to remain in the proletariat, but the freedom that each worker has to exit depends on the fact that most workers will not choose to leave. If most or all workers chose to exit from the proletariat, most would be unable to achieve their goal. Chapter 5, "Cohen on Proletarian Unfreedom," rejects this argument. Critics of Cohen have centered on the charge that collective unfreedom is unimportant. My approach, by contrast, concentrates on the structure of Cohen's argument. Cohen has not, I shall argue, proved that collective unfreedom exists.

The final chapter considers "The Socialist Alternative." Although analytical Marxists believe that socialism ought to replace capitalism, they have reached no consensus on the form of socialism that ought to be adopted. Jon Elster has devoted the most attention of the group to alternatives to capitalism, and the market socialism that he supports is analyzed in this chapter. I argue that the system of worker-controlled cooperatives that Elster favors will have little appeal to workers. Elster's claim that market socialism will better meet the need of people for creative work will also be rejected.

1

An Introduction to Analytical Marxism

The principal aim of this first chapter is to offer a brief characterization of the analytical school of Marxism. Before doing so, however, the scene must be set so that the reader can grasp what is distinctive about this school. Accordingly, the chapter first describes some of the main tenets of classical Marxism. Next, it discusses the criticisms that have led many to agree with the philosopher H. B. Acton that Marxism is a "philosophical farrago." Analytical Marxism arose as a reaction to the severe criticisms that classical Marxism had received. It attempts to reconstruct the system on a new basis.

Karl Marx believed that he had established scientific socialism. He makes such a claim repeatedly in his works—for example, in the *Communist Manifesto*, he and his collaborator Friedrich Engels contrast the positions held by their "utopian" precursors with their own views. They scorn "duodecimo editions of the New Jerusalem," and claim that the "workingmen of all countries" now (in 1848) have an exact account of the inevitable historical transition from capitalism to socialism available for their use.

Anyone may make such a claim; had Marx stopped his work with the *Manifesto*, only a few specialists would today remember his name. But he, of course, went further. In his main work, *Capital*, he attempted to set forward the "laws of motion" of capitalism. (Only Volume One of the work, published in 1867, appeared during Marx's lifetime. Engels issued Volumes 2 and 3 in 1883 and 1895; a further massive work, *The Theories of Surplus Value*, sometimes considered a final volume of *Capital*, appeared after the death of Engels under the aegis of his literary executor, Karl Kautsky.) Marx's *Capital*, replete with formulae and technical language, retreated not an inch from the assertions of the *Manifesto* that the arrival of socialism could be predicted with the inevitability of scientific law.

The outlines of Marx's theory can be quickly stated. In order to use whatever land and natural resources exist at a given time to produce profit, an economic system must find some way to extract surplus labor. Labor, in Marx's view, is the source of all value; unless laborers can produce more than they require for their subsistence, no growth in production is possible. Fortunately, workers can, on Marx's theory, generate the required surplus. For the purpose of analysis, they can be looked at as devices that, unlike ordinary machines, give rise to value. If regarded in this way, their value, like that of any other commodity, consists of the labor required to produce them. To produce but a single generation of workers, however, would avail the purchasers of labor but little. Workers must be given enough to enable them to reproduce themselves, so that the stock of labor is not exhausted. Put more simply, whatever goods enable laborers to live, continue to work, and reproduce their numbers suffice to "produce" them. Hence, on the Marxist theory, the labor required to produce these goods gives laborers their value.[1]

But *what* laborers can produce is categorically different from the labor needed to produce the goods on which the laborers live. Just as a machine can be used to create other goods than the material one requires to construct the machine, so can labor make things other than goods for its own subsistence. Further, it can produce subsistence goods in quantities beyond what is needed for laborers themselves to live on. In succinct terms, "labor power" and "labor" differ entirely. The latter is a commodity; the former, a power of producing commodities.

Labor, then, resembles a machine; on the Marxist account, however, it is a machine of a very special type. Unlike real machines, whose use in production does not in and of itself add to value, labor stands in a unique position. The difference between labor and labor power enables whoever controls labor to produce new value. Lest one be inclined to dismiss this theory out of hand, it should be noted that Marx does not deny the importance of machines. Far from it: *Capital* is not only the title but the principal subject of his *magnum opus*. But without labor, machines are sterile.

Whoever, then, controls labor occupies a fortunate position: he can secure for himself new value (Marx's technical term for this is surplus value). And this concept is more than a part of a recondite economic theory, of interest only to specialists in the history of economic thought. Quite the contrary: it is the key to Marx's entire approach to history.

After the beginning stage of history, that of "primitive communism" (the Marxist doctrine of which is found in its most elaborate form in Engels's *The Origin of the Family, Private Property, and the State*), laborers no longer control their own labor power. Instead, it has been extracted from them by a ruling class, which controls the society as far as it can to the advantage of its own members. The class that extracts the surplus, together with its manner of doing so, characterizes the various types of systems which have succeeded one another in history. These include ancient slavery, feudalism, and capitalism—the last of which, of course, occupies Marx's principal attention. The extent, if any, to which Marx thought these stages *must* succeed each other in a fixed order is a question much in dispute among Marxist exegetes.[2]

Much less in dispute than the order of the stages, however, is Marx's view of the underlying reason capitalism replaced feudalism. (Speaking of "capitalism" involves a slight if convenient anachronism, since Marx rarely refers to the system by this name.) Marx believed that there is a near constant tendency in history for the forces of production—very roughly, the technology—in a given society to expand to the greatest extent that its economic system permits. The ruling class constantly strives to extract maximum surplus value. For each level of technology, a particular social system will best promote the extraction of surplus value; it will thus tend to be established. As technology continues to develop, however, the system best fitted to the creation of surplus value changes. In Marx's vivid words, "the integument of the old order bursts," and the extant regime is replaced by a new, more productive system. For Marx, the development of capitalism out of feudalism provides the prime example of this type of transition. In the opinion of some contemporary Marxist writers—for example,

Robert Brenner and Jon Elster—this case is the only one for which Marx offers anything approaching a fully worked-out scenario.

Whatever the truth of this argument, there is no denying two points about Marx's doctrine of capitalism: he believed that its productivity vastly exceeded that of any earlier system, and he believed that its method of surplus extraction differed in a crucial way from that of any previous society.[3] The two differences, further, are not coincidental.

Slavery and feudalism extract surplus value through the use of force. Slaves and serfs who refuse to work for their masters generally suffer a dire fate: for example, in the Roman Empire, as Edward Gibbon notes, roads were sometimes lined with the crucified bodies of rebellious slaves. According to Marx, capitalism (like earlier systems) arose through violent measures; in the famous "Primitive Accumulation" chapter of the first volume of *Capital*, Marx details the many horrors that, in his opinion, led to and accompanied the rise of the new system. He places great emphasis on the causal responsibility of the slave trade and production by colonial slaves for the growth of the fortunes by which capitalism got started. His lurid descriptions of the long hours men, women, and children worked during the late eighteenth and early nineteenth centuries in Britain are well known.

Though, in origin, capitalism did not escape the violence characteristic of its predecessors, once it was established matters were quite different. The members of the working class in a capitalist system are generally *not* forced to work for any particular employers: indeed, they are free, should they so desire and can secure the means, to join the ranks of businessmen themselves. Further, contracts between workers and employers are on exactly the same basis as any other exchange.[4] Commodities exchange, roughly speaking, in proportion to their value, as determined by the labor that would be required for their production in the most socially efficient way. (Here I am using a persuasive though controversial interpretation of the labor theory by G. A. Cohen.)

On the surface, then, freedom has replaced slavery. Nevertheless, Marx insistently describes the capitalist system as one involving the exploitation of workers. At first glance, his reason for doing so is obvious. In the new system, surplus value still flows from the workers to the ruling class, in spite of the judicial principle of freedom of contract. The transfer is enabled to take place because of the fact mentioned before: labor power differs from labor. The capitalist buys the use of labor, paying what is required to produce it. So, at any rate, says the labor theory. By its purchase, the capitalist, not the worker, secures control of the instrument by which, in the phrase of the New Testament, stones are turned into bread. It is the ruling class, not the workers, that gains for its use the benefits of surplus value.

This, once more, admits of no dispute, given the truth of the premises of Marx's system. "Exploitation" just means, in Marxist terms, the surrender of surplus value—by the laborers who produce it—to the members of another class. But a deeper question now arises: given that, according to the legal system of capitalism, no one forces laborers to sell their labor to capitalists, why does Marx use the pejorative term "exploitation"? Considerable controversy has arisen in recent years over whether Marx thought that capitalism was unjust. Marx, it seems clear to me, had little use for "rights" and "justice." To him, these concepts served only to paper over the realities of capitalist production. But some scholars reject this view.[5] Whatever he thought about justice, however, he clearly disliked capitalism and eagerly looked forward to what his theory told him was inevitable: the extirpation of capitalism and its replacement by socialism. Our questions remain. Why did Marx condemn capitalism? Why is the relation between capitalists and workers best described as one of exploitation?

Two easy answers present themselves at once, only to be speedily rejected. First, Marx (as just mentioned) thought that a much better system—socialism—stood ready to replace a capitalist system that, though vastly productive, was senescent in reality. Certainly, he thought this; it does not follow, though, that a social system is exploitative because a better system will replace it. Otherwise, anyone holding that socialism will be replaced by a "higher stage" of communism would be compelled to condemn the former regime as exploitative.

Second, although Marx contended that workers were legally free, his actual portrait of British capitalism in the historical sections of *Capital* stresses entirely different features of that system. Workers, free in theory, faced death or starvation in practice were they to decline the offers of an employer. Acceptance of the "free" bargain, furthermore, often meant that workers had "voluntarily" committed themselves, their wives, and their children to working interminable hours at backbreaking labor for a mere pittance. If workers revolted, they would be brutally suppressed. (As our purpose here is a brief introductory presentation of the Marxist system, rather than an analysis, no point would be served by a discussion of whether Marx's history was accurate. It is worth mentioning, however, that many economic historians—for example, T. S. Ashton and R. M. Hartwell—present a much more sympathetic account of early capitalism than did Marx.[6])

Even if Marx's picture of early capitalism is right, our questions remain unanswered. Although Marx not only thought the lot of the worker a sorry one but believed that, until socialism arrived, it would worsen, these facts do not cut to the essence of the issue of exploitation. Marx thought the workers' sale of their labor to capitalists inherently involved exploitation, even if the conditions under which the laborer worked were not bad ones. What is the justification for such an idea?

This question introduces the principal topic of this book: the response of the analytical Marxists to the question of exploitation. Are their contentions correct? Our answer to this question will occupy much of the present work.

But before we can advance to this topic, we must complete our preliminary sketch of Marxism in its pristine form. As mentioned, Marx believed that the lot of the workers would worsen as capitalism grew to maturity: this is his well-known "immiseration" thesis. The precise details of this thesis—whether, for example, immiseration consists of a decline in absolute terms or only in an increase in inequality—are matters of controversy among interpreters.

The lot of most members of the ruling class was also an unenviable one. As technology developed, machines would force out laborers and assume an ever-greater role in the process of production. The basis for the extraction of surplus value would therefore shrink, which would bring about a tendency for the rate of profit to fall. The increasingly severe conditions necessary for the extraction of surplus value would pose a challenge to smaller capitalists that they would not be able to meet successfully. The final result would be the domination of the economy by a few great monopolistic combines.

But the group of monopolies will be no more stable than the congeries of smaller-scale firms that preceded it. Ever more severe depressions, caused by overproduction as capitalists seek by expansion to increase their profits and to destroy their rivals, will prove the rule of the day, and the proletariat—its ranks increased by those forced from the capitalist class—will of necessity be driven to revolt.

This grim account has a happy ending. When "the death-knell" of the old system sounds, a new system, vastly more productive and humane, will arise. Under it, workers will cease being exploited: they will now control their own labor and, in the form of the "dictatorship of the proletariat," rule society.

Even better things are due to arrive. The first stage of socialism will in turn be transcended, though not by violence, with a "higher stage" of socialism, in which "the free development of each will be the condition for the free development of all." (Later Marxists of strict observance—for example, Lenin and his many followers—usually use the term "communism" for this higher stage. But Marx himself does not.) Marx discusses this consummation of history at greatest length in his *Critique of the Gotha Program*; even here, though, his tone is oracular, and the reader of the tract will find little or no description of the higher stage apart from brief allusions to its desirable properties. Such is Marxism, or at any rate enough of it so that the reader can get a rough idea of what subsequent Marxists, including the group this work will endeavor to appraise, both developed and reacted against.

Some later Marxists, principally those infelicitously (though accurately) termed "Marxist-Leninists," who look to Soviet Communism with admiration, dismiss the need for any fundamental changes in the theory we have briefly presented above. V. I.

Lenin, the father of the Russian Revolution, added to Marxism an influential picture of imperialism. Otherwise, he continued to regard the scientific status of Marx's and Engels's main works as unimpeachable.[7]

More important from the standpoint of theory, G. V. Plekhanov, a Russian Marxist of strict views who strongly opposed the Bolsheviks, interpreted in *The Development of the Monist View of History* Marx's theory of history in a way that many found compelling. Further, several twentieth-century economists—for example, Ladislaus von Bortkiewicz and Maurice Dobb—refined particular phases of Marxist economics while remaining quite strictly within Marx's Ricardian tradition. (The American economist Paul Sweezy, incidentally, is *not* a case of this sort. His influential *Theory of Capitalist Development* (1942) mixes Marxist and Keynesian economics.)[8]

Even today, some writers believe that Marxism, as codified and simplified by Lenin, offers a compelling explanation of the development of capitalism. In their view, classical Marxism requires little or no change, and attacks on it invariably result from mistakes or class bias. The influential Belgian Trotskyite Ernest Mandel, in his long and learned two-volume *Marxist Economic Theory*, adds a great deal of illustration and anecdote but almost nothing of theoretical elaboration to the simplified model of Marxism presented above. Nor is Mandel's attitude based on ignorance of Marx's critics: he has recently edited a volume of essays rejecting analytical Marxist economics in favor of a view very close to that of Marx himself. And though interpretations of this kind are aberrant in the contemporary non-Communist world, they dominate the work of Marxist writers in the Soviet sphere.

In contrast to the analytical Marxists, the purists reject the criticisms which have been advanced against every major part of Marx's theory out of hand. Their views will be treated only in passing. Our main concern lies elsewhere. The distinctive feature of the analytical Marxists is precisely that, more than any other Marxist group, they take to heart the critical arguments. To see why, in their view, Marxism must be reconstructed, we must first set the scene by briefly indicating some flaws in the original system.

Even from the mere sketch of Marxism presented above, one fact is obvious. The linchpin of the entire edifice is the labor theory of value. It is this construct that lies at the basis of the notion of exploitation, an idea crucially involved in the Marxist analysis of each stage of history. Without the labor theory, how can it be argued that an exploiting class ruthlessly extracts surplus value from the laboring class, its true producer and rightful owner? Further, as already noted, the prediction of capitalism's downfall rests upon the increasing difficulty that capitalists will confront in maintaining their rate of exploitation. Once more, the labor theory seems crucial. No labor theory, no surplus value; no surplus value, no exploitation; no exploitation, no fall of capitalism.

And it is exactly the labor theory that was the focus of the most significant criticism of the system in the years after Marx's death in 1883. To begin with, economists in several countries, most notably W. S. Jevons, Léon Walras, and Carl Menger, broke with the classical tradition of value theory in which Marx wrote. Instead of asking, as the classical economists did, what objective property of goods makes them valuable, these writers placed value in the minds of consumers. Value arises from subjective preferences, not from the cost of production; included in the cost theories spurned by this group is the labor theory. It is this approach, not that of the classical economists, that nearly all subsequent economists of note have adopted. Admittedly, many economists, under the influence of Alfred Marshall, incorporated some stress upon cost-of-production into their value theory. But almost all modern economists consider the labor theory effectively dead. A contemporary defender of Marxism in its original form has the formidable task of overturning the entire corpus of modern economic theory. In this task, incidentally, the contemporary Marxist epigone cannot look to the writings of his master for help. Although the marginalist or subjective revolution in economics began in the 1870s, a decade of great intellectual activity for Marx, he failed to note its occurrence.

And the difficulty confronting the would-be strict Marxist is even more severe. The subjectivist economists did not return Marx his compliment and ignore *his* theory. Quite the contrary: Eugen von Böhm-Bawerk, Menger's chief disciple, subjected the labor theory to a total assault in his brochure *Karl Marx and the*

Close of His System and in the chapter entitled "Exploitation Theories" of his *Capital and Interest*. Böhm-Bawerk's criticisms of the labor theory were many and various.

First, he challenged the argument by which Marx arrived at the labor theory. Marx claimed that an exchange of commodities involves an equality. If, for example, one apple exchanges for two oranges, then one apple = two oranges. Marx then proceeded to inquire into the nature of this equality.

Böhm-Bawerk contended that Marx had moved too quickly. Why assume that an equality exists at all? Where exactly is it to be found? Surely not in the minds of the exchangers. The person who gives up apples for oranges prefers two oranges to one apple; the other party to the exchange has the opposite preference. Of course, given an exchange ratio, one apple is equivalent to two oranges in the trivial sense that anyone who has an apple can obtain two oranges, and vice versa. But the whole point of a theory of values is to explain the existence of an exchange ratio, so this equivalence is in itself of no use to Marx. (This issue will be discussed further in Chapter 3.)

Further, Marx claimed that the explanation of the quality he postulates cannot lie in the use values of the commodities. What someone gets from an apple or an orange is something particular: how can these values, which vary from consumer to consumer, serve as a general explanation of value?

Böhm-Bawerk countered by raising a possibility Marx had neglected. Why not look at use-value as an abstract quantity, rather than at particular use-values? Here the explanation of value would lie in both apples and oranges having use-values, not in the particular use value that each possessed. Since Marx's own theory uses labor as an abstraction, it is surprising that he neglected this analogous abstraction. Perhaps Marx's rejection of use-value to explain price has this basis. Utility consists of qualitatively different values. To say that a good is useful is not to say that a certain amount of a substance, "utility," inheres in it. How then can utility explain value? This argument assumes that a theory of prices must use a measurable concept of value. But why must it? Ludwig von Mises and other Austrians (though not Böhm-Bawerk) agree that use-value cannot be measured but explain prices without assuming otherwise.

The labor theory also failed to explain the value of land and animals used in agriculture, neither of which is the product of human labor. Some commodities gain value just by increasing in age (for example, wine and works of art): how can the labor theory explain this?

Although these criticisms were penetrating, Marxists generally failed to respond,. Another of Böhm-Bawerk's arguments, however, riveted the attention of his Marxist adversaries. The difficulty is this: according to the labor theory of value, the price of a good is determined by the amount of labor socially necessary to produce it;[9] profit is determined by the rate of surplus value. Neither proposition is true in the real world, a fact not denied by Marx. In the long run, prices equal the cost of production, rather than just the cost of labor. And the rate of profit in the economy tends to be uniform, regardless of how much labor in an industry is available for exploitation. The value of labor determines neither price nor profit. Marx aimed in the first volume of *Capital*, he said, merely to provide a simplified model. This, in true scientific fashion, would later be complicated by adding additional assumptions. This, he thought, *would* suffice to explain the prices and wages of the real world in its capitalist stage.

Unfortunately, Marx put off the solution until a later volume, and for many years after Marx's demise his followers were in a quandary, "wondering with a foolish face of praise." Engels who, as the guardian of Marx's unpublished manuscripts, alone possessed the key to the mystery—offered a prize for the best solution to the problem.

When Volume III of *Capital* finally appeared in 1895, the result was anticlimatic. Marx presented complicated calculations aimed at showing how labor values could be transformed into real-world prices and profits. Sadly for this theory, however, even if his calculations were correct (as they proved not to be),[10] they would show only that the sum of prices equalled the sum of values. That is, Marx's model in Volume III did not state that the price of each good was determined by the labor socially necessary to produce it.

Rather, he claimed that if one added up all prices in the economic system on the one hand, and all the labor values on the other, both sums would be identical. Even if Marx's equation of total prices with total values were correct, what would it prove? It seems to have little relevance to the explanation of price. Böhm-Bawerk's prescient criticism that the labor theory cannot explain actually existing market prices was triumphantly vindicated. Marx, in Volume III, had not adequately defended the labor theory.

Remember, were the labor theory to fall, the entire Marxist structure on which it rested would fall with it. As if this were not enough, critics in the century succeeding Marx's death struck at other vulnerable points of the system. Marx saw history as changing in response to the development of the forces of production. But what accounted for the growth of these forces? Concerning this, Marx says very little. Further, his depiction of "bourgeois" economics and legal theory as ideological defenses of capitalism, rather than objective sciences, rested more on assertion than argument. Marxism claimed to be *scientific* socialism—but if science carries with it the suggestion of objective proof, the claim appeared to be one that had to be taken *magna cum grano*.

The Marxists of the later nineteenth century, particularly those of Marx's own German homeland, did not ignore the criticisms to which the science of the proletariat had been subjected. In particular, Eduard Bernstein, a major voice in the Marxist Social Democratic Party and once a protégé of Engels, took to heart the increasingly troublesome predicament in which the Marxist system found itself. In *Evolutionary Socialism* (1881), Bernstein fully accepted the point that workers under an advanced capitalist economy were, *contra* Marx, better off, not worse off. This being so, the attempt at revolutionary overthrow of capitalism was doomed to certain failure. Instead, workers should, by gradual reform, transform capitalism into socialism. To Bernstein socialism *was* fully realized democracy, no more and no less.

If Bernstein and his followers jettisoned more of Marxism than anyone else who remained in the Marxist camp, they stood far from alone among their Marxist *confrères* in acknowledging the force of objections to what Engels had optimistically termed "scientific socialism." Werner Sombart, a distinguished economic historian long associated with the Social Democratic Party, hammered home the theme that the proletariat did not appear likely to take over the reins of power by the sheer weight of numbers. It did *not* represent the majority of capitalist society, but tended in a developed capitalist system to be limited to about one-third of the population.

Karl Kautsky, Engels's literary executor, responded to Marx's critics in a more orthodox way. In a major work, *The Class Struggle*, he followed Marx and Engels in predicting the inevitable downfall of capitalism. But he tended to ring the changes on the old formulas without the fire of Marx and Engels. Kautsky remained unclear throughout his long life on the exact role of party politics in expediting the "inevitable" transition to socialism: the reader of his volume will also search unsuccessfully for a clear statement on the use of revolutionary violence.

Even by the end of the nineteenth century, then, Marxism faced a theoretical challenge it seemed unable to meet. The present century has been even less kind to the scientific pretensions of Marxism; with one exception, treated immediately below, the anti-Marxist critics before the rise of the analytical school of Marxism will not be further discussed. To do so would involve too great a digression.[11]

Karl Popper, in Volume II of *The Open Society and Its Enemies* (1946), extended the work of earlier critics in a manner that has been greatly influential. A noted philosopher of science, Popper had earlier argued that the criterion of a scientific statement is falsifiability. If no conceivable empirical refutation would be accepted by a theory's proponents, the theory—though not by that fact rendered meaningless—was outside the scope of science.[12] In *The Open Society*, Popper used this criterion against Marxism: his followers never attempted an empirical test of the main predictions of the system. Marxism, whatever else it was, was *not* science.

The difficulties confronting Marxism, furthermore, were not confined to matters of theory, nor were the arguments of the doctrine's critics the sole factor leading to widespread rejection of the doctrine's scientific pretensions. On the contrary, as its Soviet acolytes never cease to remind us, Marxism is not solely a theory but a guide to action. And judged by the actions taken by the system's defenders, the doctrine was hardly a shining success. The Bolsheviks made their revolution in the name of Marxist science, but what they established was soon revealed to be an oppressive system of the worst order. Though the Soviet system is not without its contemporary apologists (a recent example is Richard Miller, *Analyzing Marxism* (1985)), most Western Marxists theorists distanced their system from existing Communist reality. Soviet totalitarianism, argued eminent social democrats such as Sidney Hook, was *not* what Marx wanted.[13]

Suppose that Hook and his fellow Marxist revisionists were right. Marxism, judged as a theory of the actual world, still faces grave difficulties. Many propositions intrinsic to the system seem straight-forwardly false. We have already dealt with the labor theory; further, the many hostages Marx gave to fortune by his prediction of the future course of history seemed to unravel the system even further, as more and more time elapsed while they remained unfulfilled. The condition of the proletariat did *not* worsen in the major Western economies: it improved enormously. There has *not* been an ever-increasing trend toward monopoly domination. Social-ism did *not* first arise in a highly industrialized country, as the theory would lead one to expect.[14] Most important, the much-promised collapse of capitalism seems far away. Perhaps Popper erred—in that Marxism is not unfalsifiable, but false.

The manner in which Marxists responded to these trends, as well as to the critical analysis that accompanied them, did not suffice to win them many converts. One school, that of Soviet Marxism, simply repeated the old claims.[15] The Trotskyite sub-species of Marxism did little better. Leon Trotsky, a writer of powerful intellect and slashing style, was the most famous advo-cate of the doctrine of "permanent revolution." A Marxist revolution might arise in a backward country like Russia—but unless it was supported quickly by revolutions in the advanced countries of Europe, socialism established at the "weakest link" of the chain of capitalism would face imminent collapse. Though he was original in this belief, Trotsky in his immense *corpus* devoted little attention to the Marxist analysis of exploitation that holds center stage in this book. Rather, he took its truth for granted. His followers (for example, the aforementioned Ernest

Mandel) have in this respect proved faithful acolytes of their leader. Since they leave the main body of Marxist theory largely where they find it, Trotsky and other leaders of his Fourth International will in this work be passed over.

Responding to the difficulties in another way, many Western Marxists shifted their interest in Marxism from its scientific claims to its philosophy. In a trend inaugurated by Georg Lukács, *History and Class-Consciousness* (the Hegelian commentaries of Marx's youth) now stood in the center of attention. Marxism was no longer considered a science; it was now revealed to have been a philosophical system concerned with the analysis of alienation all along. Hegelian philosophy, as everyone knows, is hardly distinguished by its lucidity; the immensely detailed discussions of concepts found in Marx's early manuscripts by Lukács, Theodor Adorno, Max Horkheimer, Lucio Colletti, and many others can be fully grasped only by someone willing to immerse himself in a bizarre and hermetic terminology. Fortunately, that is not our task here.

Before turning to the main theme of this work, however, a further development of what might pejoratively be called hermetic Marxism needs to be discussed. Max Horkheimer and Theodor Adorno have already been mentioned. Together with several others, some of whom (for example, Erich Fromm and Herbert Marcuse) later achieved fame in the United States, they established an Institute for Social Research under the aegis of the University of Frankfurt. Though some members of the school—such as Karl-August Wittfogel—engaged in empirical research, Horkheimer and Adorno usually did not. Instead, they subsumed Marxism under what Adorno called "negative dialectics." By this term, they intended to indicate that true social criticism rejects what ordinary science, both physical and social, considers to be facts. To accept the empirical world as it appears to the ordinary observer is to render oneself complicit with a repressive social order. In their joint venture, *Dialectic of Enlightenment*, written when the Institute—in fear of Nazi persecution—had moved to Columbia University, reason itself (as understood by the Enlightenment) stood indicted for insinuating into society the evils of technological domination. I fear that the views of the school may yet remain opaque to those readers not previously acquainted with them. This is in large part as Adorno and Horkheimer would desire things, since they also spurned easy intelligibility as superficial and pro-capitalist.

Small wonder that non-Marxists—faced with the apparent theoretical and empirical collapse of Marxism and the retreat of many leading Marxist theorists to a type of philosophy considered by contemporary philosophers to be long outmoded—often suspected that Marxism was neither science nor philosophy but religion. Eric Voegelin and Arnold Toynbee forcefully pressed this appraisal of Marxism: it is to be found in its best-argued and most comprehensive form in Leszek Kolakowski's massive three-volume *Main Currents of Marxism*.

In the opinion of the Frankfurt School, then, Marxism was not a science. A group of French Marxists headed by Louis Althusser clashed hand-on with the Frankfurt School. They insisted that Marx *should* be read as advancing scientific claims. But this group, while translating Marxist views into a complicated terminology of their own devising, did not refute the leading criticisms of Marx that we have briefly discussed. How could it? Its members did not even note the existence of non-Marxists; instead, they devoted their time to an elaboration of Marx's concepts of "determination" and similar topics.

So the situation stood until the late 1960s and early 1970s. Marxism appeared finished, at least to those whose tastes ran neither to Soviet apologetics, Hegelian philosophy, nor neoscholasticism of the Althusserian sort. But, like a phoenix risen from the ashes, Marxism once again confronts us as a powerful intellectual system. So, at any rate, a new group of scholars—the so-called analytical Marxists—contends. Their doctrines are the subject of the remainder of this book. Before examining their contentions in detail in subsequent chapters, we shall briefly discuss how the movement arose, who its dominant actors are, and the nature of its chief contentions. As we begin this task, one *caveat*: the writers we have to consider form no monolithic school in the style of Leninism and Trotskyism. They frequently argue among themselves, and often the best criticisms of doctrines professed by one analytical Marxist can be found in the work of another. Unless otherwise noted, then, particular views should be attributed only to the writer then being discussed.

We now approach our main topic. Several scholars in the late 1960s viewed the dubious intellectual standing of Marxism neither as something to be accepted and despaired of nor as a matter to be ignored. Instead, it presented an obstacle to be overcome. If Marxism did not meet the highest intellectual standards, it must be overhauled so that it might do so. If it was not yet science, a job of reconstruction was obviously on the agenda. This Herculean task was to be accomplished principally through the aid of two disciplines, economics and analytical philosophy, both of which were characterized by high standards of precision and technical elaboration. By applying the techniques of these disciplines to Marxism, it was hoped, a substantial theory that was both rigorous and recognizably Marxist could be constructed.

As even Macaulay's schoolboy knows, modern economics possesses a high degree of analytic rigor. At least since Paul Samuelson's *Foundations of Economic Analysis* (1948), most mainstream economists have spun endless mathematical models of the economy. The majority of the practictioners of these exercises have ignored Marxism; but, as will be discussed in the next few pages, several economists are both rigorously trained mathematicians and Marxists. They challenge the remainder of the economics profession with the claim that, applying the techniques generally recognized in the discipline, large elements of the Marxist system emerge "bloody, but unbowed." If they are right, standard economists will be unable to ignore Marxist claims any longer.

A similar situation arises in philosophy, the principal area on which this book concentrates. At the turn of the twentieth century, idealism of a roughly Hegelian sort dominated the philosophical world, at least in its British and American sectors. Philosophers such as F. H. Bradley, Bernard Bosanquet, and Josiah Royce, who are seldom studied today, were then names to conjure with. Though these writers were by no means inept, they tended to advance vague claims about the world, the arguments for which proved difficult to pin down. What, for example, Bosanquet meant by the "concrete universal" or Royce by the "community of interpretation" would probably defeat even the most patient expositor's efforts to explain clearly and simply.

A number of philosophers at the turn of the century, most importantly Bertrand Russell and G. E. Moore, reacted strongly against idealist philosophy in the style of Bradley and Bosanquet. Dismissing it as woolly Hegelianism, they spurned system-building and efforts to compress the cosmos into an explanatory formula. Instead, they began to analyze particular arguments with unparalleled precision. For these philosophers, exact discrimination of concepts was the key to the kingdom, and all the practitioners of analytic philosophy aim to follow the motto of Russell's greatest pupil, Ludwig Wittgenstein, in his *Tractatus:* "Whatever can be said, can be said clearly."

Critics of analytic philosophy (for example, Herbert Marcuse), sometimes dismiss the movement as a venture in triviality. But regardless of what one thinks of it, this style of philosophy is by far the most influential type practiced today in the leading universities of Britain and America. Analytical Marxism advances the bold and far reaching claim that not only modern economics but also contemporary analytic philosophy can be applied to Marxism. Once more, if the analytical Marxists can make out their case, analytic philosophers, few of whom have any interest in Marxism, will be compelled to change their attitude. No longer will economists and philosophers, if analytical Marxism holds up, be able to dismiss Marxism as outmoded Hegelianism.

At first sight, the claim that analytic philosophy can contribute to Marxism appears surprising. That discipline is characterized by an unwavering respect for formal logic. Yet Marx was an Hegelian; to Hegel, formal logic was a minor and inconsequential matter, an affair of the mere Understanding. True philosophical thinking, by contrast, is dialectical.[16] In this opinion, he was assiduously followed by Engels (principally in the *Anti-Dühring* and *Dialectics of Nature*) and, though at much less length, by Marx himself.

But the analytical Marxists will have nothing of this. Instead, a good test to follow if in doubt whether a particular writer supports the analytic school is to see whether he mentions dialectics with favor. If he does, he must immediately be crossed off the list.

Even to cite the word at all counts against membership in the analytic school.

The analytical movement began when several economists attempted the paradoxical task of constructing a Marxist science of economics without the labor theory of value. This sounds like Hamlet without the Danish prince, but perhaps this is only a false appearance. If one could construct an economic theory that demonstrated the inevitable downfall of capitalism while still working within the classical tradition from which Marx sprang, did it really matter whether one preserved the labor theory?

To one economist, Ian Steedman of the University of Manchester, it clearly did not matter. In *Marx after Sraffa* (1977), following a number of earlier journal articles, he mounted a slashing attack on the labor theory, arguing that it was totally unsound. Like Böhm-Bawerk, he insisted that Marx had completely failed to derive a realistic account of capitalist prices and wages from his simplified model in Volume I of *Capital*. Further, even the simple model of that volume is deficient on its own terms. Its explanation of the value of labor power is fatally infected with circularity.

Instead of the labor theory, Steedman wished to rely on a complex cost-of-production theory developed by the Italian economist Piero Sraffa, a famed teacher at Cambridge University and a close friend of both Keynes and Wittgenstein. In his *Production of Commodities by Means of Commodities,* a brief but forbiddingly complex monograph, Sraffa developed a way of calculating the prices of commodities by reference to a particular commodity as a standard. This theory, in Steedman's opinion, was the pearl of great price enabling one to achieve the task that had proved to be beyond Marx—the construction of a valid objective theory of value. We need not enter into the details of Sraffa's system, as Steedman developed it, here: some of the views of Sraffa and Steedman will be described in Chapter III below. Regardless of the technical merits of this approach, however, it raises a central difficulty for Marxism which will be a principal topic of this book. We shall see what that difficulty is in a moment.

Before turning to it, it should be noted that Steedman's rejection of the labor theory is no aberration. The entire analytic school concurs in consigning it to the dustbin of fallacious theory. Jon Elster, a Norwegian polymath who is one of the three main analytic Marxists we shall be discussing, has summed up the view of the labor theory common among the analytic school in this way: "I argue that the theory is useless at best, harmful and misleading at its not infrequent worst."[17]

As suggested previously, this view of the labor theory, however indisputable on the ground of economic theory, raises a severe problem for Marxism. If Marxism is to survive bereft of the labor theory, it clearly must still be able to contend on other grounds that all history, and capitalism in particular, rests upon the exploitation of labor, and that only the arrival of socialism will end exploitation. And how can Marxism prove exploitation without the labor theory?

This difficulty cannot be solved by defying economics and returning to the labor theory, as has been pointed out with characteristic acuity by G. A. Cohen, a Canadian philosopher and political theorist who is now Professor of Social and Political Theory at All Souls College, Oxford, after a long sojourn at the University of London. Cohen notes that even if one accepts the labor theory of value, it still seems difficult for the Marxist to show that capitalism exploits workers. The labor theory, Cohen argues, does not contend that the value of a good is the labor that produces it—on *this* view, Cohen thinks, it *would* be natural to think that a system that deprives workers of control of the goods whose value they have alone created must of necessity rest on exploitation. Rather, the theory claims that the value of a good is the socially necessary time that *would be* required to produce it. It is not at all intuitively obvious, on this interpretation, why workers who must sell their labor to capitalists are exploited: why should the actual producers be entitled to what *would* be produced under other conditions? Does the Marxist argument for capitalist exploitation fail because of a simple mistake in modality—the confusion of *would have* produced and *did* produce?

Cohen does not think that the Marxist claim does fail, and his contribution as an analytical Marxist far exceeds emphasizing a refinement of the labor theory. He has shifted the entire focus of the debate over Marxist exploitation in a way that makes him the single most important figure to be considered in this book.

To previous Marxists, whether or not they accepted the labor theory, the central issue in the discussion of exploitation was one of economics. How was the exploitative nature of capitalism—a matter taken for granted as an assumption rather than proved as a conclusion—best to be explained? The economic issue interests Cohen, but it has not been his main area of work. As he has realized more adequately than any previous Marxist, the issue of exploitation is first of all a matter not for economics but for political philosophy. *Why* is it a case for condemnation that most workers in a capitalist economy sell their labor to capitalists?

In confronting this problem, Cohen has faced head-on the fundamental paradox confronting anyone who thinks that capitalists exploit workers. We have already mentioned it earlier in this chapter, in the discussion of Marx's theory of history. Workers are not coerced into working for capitalists. With perfect legal freedom, they may form cooperatives or start individual businesses of their own. How, then, are they exploited? Cohen argues that workers are "collectively unfree" to leave the proletariat; his claim to this effect will be examined in detail in Chapter 5 below.

Cohen's assault on capitalism rests on much more than the controversial notion of collective unfreedom. He attempts to undermine the foundations of capitalism directly by a criticism of the justice of individual ownership of the means of production. His criticism takes the form of a detailed analysis and rejection of the theory of justice defended in Robert Nozick's *Anarchy, State, and Utopia*, widely considered the most sophisticated defense of a regime of pure capitalism. His criticism of Nozick will be considered in a later chapter. The argument of the present book stands or falls, more than on any other issue, with the contention that Cohen has failed to undermine the case for the justice of capitalism.

Cohen's path in concentrating on political philosophy was completely unexpected when compared with the way earlier Marxist theorists had argued. He even further braved the perils of non-conformity by directly contradicting a cherished belief and practice of Marx himself. As earlier mentioned, much controversy has arisen in the past few years over whether Marx thought that capitalism was unjust. (Cohen, not surprisingly, holds that he did.) But even if Marx did have a distinctive approach to justice, it is one that very much stands to the side in his mature works. As we have already illustrated, the analysis of economics, not ethical theory, stands at the core of Marx's own work. Cohen dares to abandon the characteristic Marxist denigration of political and ethical theory as at best peripheral, at worst ideological.

The impression so far given of Cohen's approach may create a misunderstanding. Although Cohen practices analytical ethics to an extent undreamed-of by earlier Marxists, his ultimate goal is not to abandon the deterministic view of history distinctive of classical Marxism for a voluntaristic picture of people arriving at the best society through rational argument. His greatest claim to fame, in fact, is his *Karl Marx's Theory of History—A Defence,* in which the skill of a first-rate analytic philosopher is used to defend an interpretation of Marx's view very similar to Plekhanov's. In Cohen's view, the growth of the forces of production, long a mystery to be accepted without question by the Marxist faithful, could be explained rationally. To do so, Cohen argued, one must postulate a near-constant motive of people at all stages of history to expand production as much as possible. Whether this desire is in fact, as Cohen thinks it is, something that counts as a historical constant is an open question. But his position, at any rate, is neither ridiculous nor implausible; he has thus scored a major victory for the Marxist position in rendering the erstwhile inexplicable understandable. Among the book's manifold riches is an argument directed against H. B. Acton, a leading critic of Marxism, that the distinction between forces and relations of production can be drawn in a non-circular way. Most controversially, the book defends against many philosophers of science the validity of a type of functional explanation Cohen deems essential to the Marxist position. In brief, Cohen contends that the relations of production change because doing so will advance the growth of the forces of production. This advance is the "function" of the change. Elster, among others, has harshly criticized this type of explanation by purpose.

The preceding paragraph counts as a digression, allowable in order to give the reader an idea of the scope and nature of Cohen's concerns. But our central topic in this book is not Marx's theory of history, but the analytic school's views on exploitation under capitalism and socialism. Here Cohen's characteristic approach, while influential, by no means defines the position of the whole school. A different though related view of exploitation has been advanced in a number of books and articles by the American economist John Roemer, now teaching at the University of California at Riverside. The most important of his works for our purposes are his *General Theory of Exploitation and Class* (1982) and two articles in the journal *Philosophy and Public Affairs* appearing in 1982 and 1985.

Like many other contemporary economists, Roemer's pages are heavily laced with mathematics. Indeed, the non-economist cannot help but feeling that Roemer's books consist of one equation after another, interrupted by an occasional prose remark. But the situation, even for the non-mathematical reader, is not nearly so bad as it seems. Most of the equations elaborate what are actually simple and straightforward ideas. Like Cohen and Elster, he consigns the labor theory of value to the scrapheap and wishes to find a new basis from which to argue that capitalism is exploitative.

Unlike Cohen, he does not repair to the realm of philosophy for his notion of exploitation; he remains (mostly, at least) within his own discipline of economics. But unlike Marx, Roemer does not derive exploitation from the process of production. The exploitation of labor, so much stressed by all previous Marxists, is but the deeper consequence of something else. This underlying cause is the differential ownership of capital assets—one class alone in a typical capitalist society tends to own all the important capital goods, to the virtual exclusion from effective power over the capital of anyone else. To Roemer, this situation is itself exploitative. It further explains the more usual type of exploitation in the following way. If some people own capital goods and others do not, Roemer argues that those who do not will find it to their advantage to work for those better equipped than themselves with capital. Classes, understood in the Marxist way, will emerge.

Roemer claims to prove all this rigorously, through mathematical analysis of several models each more complex than the one preceding it in the series.

As we shall see in detail in a subsequent chapter, Roemer's concept of exploitation is quite odd. Under it, even a worker who is not forced to work for a capitalist, but very much wants to do so because this will be best for him, counts as exploited. In fact, as Roemer himself notes, exploitation in his system can occur even if no one works for anyone else.

Why does Roemer adopt so Pickwickian a concept of exploitation? As we shall see, he does so because he believes that without the equal distribution of capital assets, free economic exchange leads to unjust results. Unfortunately, he deploys little in the way of argument for this claim—just how little will be seen in detail in the chapter that covers his views. (In a later chapter, furthermore, I shall endeavor to show that even in a society that begins with the equal ownership of capital, it would be rational for people to establish capitalist firms in which some people worked for others.) Roemer's arguments against capitalism, I shall contend, entirely fail in their purpose.

The third of the triumvirate of analytic Marxists whose views will be analyzed at length in this book has already been briefly cited. He is the Norwegian social and political theorist Jon Elster. He writes with a method and manner all his own; in his books, argument cascades after argument, accompanied by displays of wide learning in many fields. But although he has views on an enormous variety of issues, he is not associated with a distinct thesis in the style of Cohen and Roemer. His large-scale work on Marxism, *Making Sense of Marx* (1985), deserves discussion not principally for a new conception it advances of its subject, but more for a key fact about the analytic school Elster brings out better than anyone else.

The fact in question, one suspects, was not one Elster aimed to establish; quite the contrary, one may be sure he would sharply reject it if used to characterize his book. Nevertheless, the point we have in mind emerges clearly from the book. It is that very little remains of Marxism when Elster and his colleagues are finished analyzing and "defending" it. Elster rejects the labor theory of value, Marx's theory of capitalist crisis, the application of historical materialism to Greek and Roman antiquity, most of Marx's class theory, and the Marxist theory of ideology. He does like Marx's portrayal of the capitalist factory, holding it to be an excellent sociological description. He also (in contrast to nearly everyone else) thinks Marx was a methodological individualist (i.e., someone who believes that a complete analysis of society must explain all social states by referring only to the motives and behavior of the individuals who compose it); he praises him for adopting this position in at least some of his work. Though he insists he is a Marxist, he has little in common with the founder of that doctrine besides an antipathy towards capitalism.

Though most members of the analytic school do not go as far as Elster in gainsaying so many parts of the original system, they all reject essential elements of the classical picture. We shall see that when all the criticisms are put together, analytical Marxism becomes a formidable weapon in the hands of anti-Marxists. As an instrument for a Marxist renaissance, it fails.

Although Cohen, Elster, and Roemer are the principal figures discussed here, they do not exhaust the membership of the analytic school. To enable the reader to get a better idea of the scope of the group, a few others should be mentioned, although they will not be discussed further in this book.

The sociologist Erik Olin Wright has applied the techniques of game theory to the analysis of class: he has also been strongly influenced by Roemer's notion of exploitation. Robert Brenner, a historian whose work on the transition from feudalism to capitalism has won him much fame, is usually classed with the analytic school. Although he does not contradict their views, his work does not commit itself to any particular tenets distinctive of the school. The philosophers William Shaw and Allen Wood have advocated models of Marx's historical scheme similar to those of G. A. Cohen.

Another American philosopher, Joshua Cohen, has subjected G. A. Cohen's account of Marx to sharp criticism; he has also analyzed the working of American democracy in a fashion that has won him Elster's praise. Three American philosophers, Andrew Levine, Donald Little, and Richard Miller, have written accounts of Marx that are both analytically sophisticated and sympathetic.

David Schweickart, trained both as an economist and a philosopher, has written an important work defending workers' cooperatives. His criticism of capitalism will be addressed in a later chapter. Further, in addition to Roemer, a number of other economists, including Michio Morishima and Ian Steedman, have used modern mathematical techniques to refine and develop Marxist economics.

The preceding rather breathless survey is, of course, not intended as an adequate presentation of the work of any of the people mentioned. Rather, it is intended to indicate to the reader that much more is going on among analytic Marxists than will be discussed in this book. Further, by speaking of an analytic "school," I do not mean that the persons mentioned adhere to a monolithic creed. Rather, the group consists of a loose association of people united only by their use of modern philosophy or economics to analyze Marxism.

2

The Classical Marxist Assault
on Capitalism

I

In the present chapter, an argument intended to show that capitalism is a just economic system will be developed. The principal Marxist response to this argument—namely, that capitalism rests on exploitation of the working class—will then be considered. This response will be the subject of much of the rest of this book; in this chapter, an overview of the reasons for rejecting it will be given. We shall conclude that the argument favoring the justice of capitalism survives the Marxist criticism of it.

Before an argument concerning capitalism can be presented, a definition of that system is obviously needed. For the purposes of this chapter, capitalism will be defined as a developed economy in which most, or all, of the principal means of production are privately owned, and in which no central planning agency attempts to coordinate the economic system.

Several features of this definition require comment. First, a developed economy has been specified to conform with the Marxist view that capitalism arises only when the forces of production have reached a high stage of growth.[1] Second, private ownership of the main means of production is not by itself a sufficient condition for capitalism. Fascist economic systems for example, combine private ownership with detailed regulation by the state of the way production is to be carried out.[2] Such an economy does not come within the purview of the argument to be presented below supporting the practice of capitalism. Third, the central agency is said to "attempt" to coordinate the economy in order not to beg the question against those who believe no central planning agency can attain its goal of detailed regulation of a viable economy without the assistance of some other method of economic calculation. Ludwig von Mises, Friedrich Hayek, and other Austrian economists contend that a socialist system cannot work in a developed economy. Without a market, they hold, it is (nearly) impossible to decide how to produce capital goods efficiently. Thus, existing "socialist" regimes do not operate completely through central planning.[3] (Agencies such as the U. S. Federal Reserve Board, though of great importance, do not make a system possessing them non-capitalist by the present definition. They do not regulate the economy in detail.)

The points about the definition given so far seem safely non-controversial. Nevertheless, the definition does have several features that one suspects will move the Marxist to protest, claiming that we have begged the question against him from the start. First, it contains no requirement that a distinct class of proletarians—persons whose income exclusively, or almost exclusively, rests on labor under owners of the means of production— exists, let alone that it be essential to the operation of the economy. Second, no special class of owners of the means of production is assumed to exist. Moreover, no requirement is made that capitalism begin in a certain way; for all that the definition mandates, a capitalist economy could have begun with the world's creation. A Marxist, it is clear, will not take those items as uncontroversial.

In his view, of course, exactly those items excluded from the definition are essential to capitalism. A developed capitalist economy, for reasons sketched out in the Introduction, consists of two principal classes: capitalists (that is, owners of the means of production) and proletarians. Further, the existing capitalist system arose in a particular fashion that is greatly relevant to its present nature. It did not come into being through the agreement of rational contractors with legitimate claims to their resources. Rather, its tainted origins lie in slavery and feudal exploitation. Does the definition then assume that Marxism is false?

Not at all. It remains perfectly open to the Marxist to demonstrate that capitalism, as above defined, does have the characteristics he postulates. The definition does not assume that the Marxist point of view is incorrect; instead, it attempts a neutral characterization. In John Rawls's useful distinction, the definition tries to arrive at the concept of capitalism, instead of offering a conception—a point of view—of it.[4] To place Marxist doctrines within the definition would be to beg the question in favor of that system.

Our hypothetical Marxist might argue that the definition begs the question against Marxism in a subtler way. Marxists contend that their view of the historical origins of capitalism is not mere extraneous detail. Quite the contrary: the object of study when capitalism is under consideration is the existing system, not some philosopher's ideological model of that system. Whether it is logically possible to imagine a capitalist system without exploitation is a scholastic conundrum, given that actually existing capitalism rests on exploitation. Once more, though we shall indeed be pursuing just the "scholastic" inquiry that Marxists reject, the definition does not beg the question against their view of the way capitalism originated. It leaves open all historical inquiries into the origins of capitalism, as well as not mandating any specific method of inquiry into capitalism. The definition allows one to be as "abstract" or as historical as one wishes. As we shall see below, the analytical Marxists tend to press the argument against abstract, non-historical analysis much less than most other Marxists do.[5]

If our definition has survived thus far, it now confronts a much more difficult problem. We proposed to construct a *prima facie* argument for the justice of capitalism. But what is justice? Here a mere appeal to a commonly-held concept will not work; the topic of the criteria of justice is one of the most controversial in contemporary philosophy.[6] How, then, are we to proceed? Obviously, it will not do simply to adopt one's favorite theory of justice and declare the justice of capitalism vindicated. But the resolution of the problem does not require so drastic a "solution." Once more, the key lies in an appeal to neutrality and to limited claims. *Other things being equal*, it is suggested, a just economic system is one in which people are free to make any economic arrangements they wish, so long as they do not coerce others. Contrary to the initial impression it creates, this standard is one most socialists should find acceptable. It is perfectly allowable for a socialist to say that one of the "other things that must be equal" is that his preferred method of production and distribution be instituted. Most socialists attach *some* value to freedom to engage in economic exchange: this is all the standard requires. Jon Elster, for example, recognizes as a "powerful objection" to socialism that it might have to forbid people from forming capitalist firms.[7]

Before testing capitalism by this proposed standard, a good deal of preliminary work needs to be done. It is hardly likely that Marxists (and non-Marxist critics of capitalism) will accept the claim that this criterion of a just economic system is, in fact, neutral. Unlike our definition of capitalism, it does indeed appear nonneutral. Isn't capitalism precisely the system in which people are free to make any exchanges they wish—in contrast to socialism, in which a pattern of activity is prescribed for people? Therefore, isn't the criterion suggested just a way of making it true by definition that capitalism is a just system?

As one might anticipate, our subsequent discussion will answer "no" to this question. We must discuss several parts of the criterion, however, to evaluate properly the points at stake. The simplest of these concerns one phrase: "people are free to make any economic arrangements they wish." This means that mutual consent is required for an agreement. That is, no claim is advanced that, in a just social system, each person can secure any economic benefit he wishes. It is surely utopian (in a negative sense) to advance as a criterion of justice that each person who, for example, wishes to have the standard of living enjoyed by a multimillionaire is able to do so. Instead, what is meant is that any two or more people who mutually agree on terms are free to exchange any goods or services in their rightful possession. Anyone *can*, under capitalism, enjoy the standard of life of a multi-millionaire—provided that he can find one or more other people willing to pay or give him the requisite money. If the mere desire of one individual is not enough for him to achieve his goals, neither is anything more than mutual non-coercive agreement required. In particular, no one besides the individuals concerned need agree: there is no demand that all individuals in the society accept the proposed change. (This also holds true for a majority of all individuals, a majority of individuals affected by a transaction, etc.) Below, we will consider a criticism of the criterion on the grounds that it is insufficiently restrictive in this regard: for now, it is simply posited.

A much more difficult problem arises from the requirement that proposed economic changes be non-coercive. As is well known, the definition of coercion presents many snags for the unwary; the best available treatment, contained in an article by Robert Nozick, arrives—after intricate analysis and ingenious counter-example—at a result of great complexity.[8] Fortunately for our purposes, the commonsense definition of coercion, "force or the threat of force," meets our needs. Not that coercion is unimportant; as we shall soon see, much of the analytical Marxist criticism of capitalism involves reference to that system's alleged coercion of workers. But the Marxist case does not turn on the use of a hyper-refined definition of coercion, and in this instance we need not depart from common sense.

The phrase "other things being equal" cannot be fully explained before we present the argument for capitalism and consider the Marxist criticisms of it. Before we can proceed, however, it must be unpacked to some extent. What is meant is not that freedom of exchange must be accepted by everyone as an unchallengeable principle of justice, nor that freedom of exchange as the sole criterion for the evaluation of an economic system is a neutral one, alike in being acceptable to both Marxists and their critics. Rather, all that the criterion claims is that freedom to make non-coercive economic arrangements is an advantage in terms of justice to any system possessing it. That is to say, items other than freedom of this sort favored by some theorists—for example, "positive freedom," social solidarity, economic security, lack of alienation, etc.—must be weighed against freedom of exchange if they form part of a social system that lacks this kind of freedom. Further, it is assumed that economic freedom, if it exists, is important. Obviously, if a system allowed economic freedom but such freedom was an inconsequential matter, the fact that, "other things being equal," it was a good system would not count for much.

To reiterate, we have not begged the question in favor of capitalism. If, as argued below, it turns out that capitalism possesses the feature singled out by the criterion and its rivals do not, this by no means commits us to acknowledging that capitalism is the only just system or that it outranks all other systems in this quality. It is only that, in the indicated circumstance, those who wish to argue that capitalism is not just (or that some other system is morally better) need to weigh the desirable features their system possesses (and capitalism does not) against capitalist economic freedom in their assessment of the justice of economic systems. The relevant feature can, of course, be the absence of a defect that capitalism is alleged to posses. But we have a long way to go before arriving at this conclusion.

One more preliminary point requires a modicum of attention. In speaking of the "justice" of an economic system, a wide sense of that term is being used. It is intended to be a general term of moral evaluation—no contrast with other moral terms such as "goodness" or "welfare-promoting" is meant. This point is important because, as we shall see in a subsequent chapter, a principal defense of capitalism revolves around the claim that capitalism is demanded by a system of rights. In this theory, that of the philosopher Robert Nozick, the justice of a system—that is, its adherence to the proper scheme of rights—is explicitly contrasted with its effects on welfare. But this distinction will only concern us later. We may now turn to the argument for the *prima facie* justice of capitalism.

With the preliminary work of explaining the criterion out of the way, the actual argument is simple and straightforward. Under a capitalist system, people in fact are free to exchange in the indicated way. The point is hardly a controversial one: Marx, in the course of condemning capitalism, admits that in contrast to slavery and feudalism, workers are formally free to make whatever wage bargains they wish under capitalism.[9] He holds this, however, to be of little or no importance, for reasons we shall consider below. And it is even less controversial that non-workers under capitalism can enter into the economic arrangements they wish. Of course, it need not follow from the fact than an opponent of capitalism concedes that it has some good features that the system in fact possesses them—perhaps the opponents underestimate the strength of their case. But not in the present instance: the point at issue is built into the definition of capitalism we have presented. To show that capitalism does not have this feature, it would be necessary for the objector to show that the definition we have given leads to a contradiction.

To revert to a point referred to earlier, it would not be sufficient for an objector to claim that existing capitalism lacks this feature. In fact, most analytical Marxists do not claim this, but one can readily imagine an objector who does—claiming that workers either *must* accept, in general, the terms of trade proposed to them by capitalists or else face suppression by force. Even if this were true, the argument for capitalism as we have defined it would not be affected. The actually existing system would not qualify as "capitalism" on the definition given: the historical point about the existing system would therefore be irrelevant. It is, in particular, irrelevant to rehearse stories (stories, in point of fact, of question-able veracity)[10] about the horrors of the Industrial Revolution, unless it can be shown that such conditions are intrinsically necessary to the capitalist system.

And to prove this, an objector unable to meet the challenge of proving that any system of private ownership of the means of production *must* involve lack of economic freedom should at least show that any system that began as acceptably capitalist by the terms of our definition must inevitably degenerate into a regime without economic freedom.

Some might object that so broad and ambitious a task is unnecessary. Suppose that a critic of capitalism could show that, in the circumstances of capitalism's actual development, workers or other economic actors lacked economic freedom. Should we not be studying this—that is, the existing history and sociology of capitalism—rather than an abstract model of how the system *might* work?

To this complaint, no decisive reply will be attempted: the usefulness, or lack of it, of the sort of logical analysis being attempted here will emerge from the discussion. It is, at any rate, not a criticism characteristic of the analytical Marxists: Cohen, Elster, and Roemer engage in precisely the type of logical analysis attempted here. And regardless of one's estimate of the place of historical study, the procedure of the analytic school seems reasonable. In the absence of a study of the concepts involved, how can one know whether particular features of a system are necessary or accidental to it? If it is replied (as some Marxists would) that the distinction between conceptual analysis and historical fact is an unreal one, because the development of history through certain stages is itself inevitable, *this* has to be shown by logical argument, not just by appeal to historical example. And the arguments in question, if they are not to count as mere variations of the conceptual analysis undertaken here, must not depend on assumptions about the way a system of private enterprise would logically have to work. Although the analytical Marxists have not eschewed conceptual analysis, the present discussion is not irrelevant. As we shall endeavor to show in later chapters, the analytical Marxists do assume the truth of controversial and contingent historical propositions at various points in their discussion of the logic of capitalism.[11]

To show that the type of argument offered in support of capitalism is not misguided on its face does not suffice to defend the particular argument presented from direct assault on its premises. An obvious line of attack lies in denying the premise that economic freedom is, other things being equal, a moral advantage, and an important one, to the system that has it. It might be contended that people's choices are of little or no value unless they choose the "right" things. Allan Gilbert, following what appears to be the teaching of Mao Tse-tung, suggests that only choices that relate to sets of basic human needs are important: the freedom to choose as one wishes beyond those needs is at best an irrelevance, and at worst a discreditable feature of capitalism.[12] Less drastically, it might be argued that freedom of economic choice is indeed desirable—but only in a particular environment in which people are in a position to choose rationally. In present-day capitalist society, people are subject to constant bombardment that induces them to make irrational purchases. In the final stage of communism, and perhaps in certain stages of socialism before that happy consummation, freedom of choice will be a good, but not until then. This position is not, of course, merely a conjectural line of approach; it was famously advocated by Herbert Marcuse.[13]

The two variant positions have been presented only to receive rather short shrift. The more extreme version—that is, that freedom of choice is morally desirable only if exercised upon a very limited set of needs—is one that few readers will find plausible. The view that people do not know what is good for them but must be "educated" to respond only to certain needs seems unacceptably paternalistic. It contravenes assumptions about the desirability of freedom that are shared not only by those in the classical liberal tradition but also by the analytical Marxists: Jon Elster, especially, has been much concerned with the desirability of freedom of choice. Admittedly, the above remarks do not constitute an argument against the paternalistic contention: we have merely claimed that the position is not widely shared and is, for those at all influenced by liberalism, implausible. But further argument on this point is really a matter for another work. The advocate of the "needs" position has the unenviable task of supplying a complete list of acceptable needs and then arguing that choice has moral value only for items on that list.

As to the less extreme Marcusean position, once more we stand faced with a particular historical claim about existing capitalist society. Unless Marcuse has an argument to show that capitalism *must* be characterized by propaganda and conditioning of the sort he opposes, his analysis, whatever its intrinsic interest, has no relevance for us.[14]

We may go one step further. Even if it could be shown that conditioning of the sort Marcuse discusses *does* inevitably occur under capitalism, our criterion of justice would not be affected. The criterion forbids only coercive activities, understood in the strict sense of the use or threat of force. All other types of economic activity are allowed: nothing specifically prohibits the use of propaganda.

But is not the system of propaganda, painted in despairing colors by Marcuse, an obviously undesirable one? If it could be shown that capitalism must result in this sort of propaganda, would this not be a grave count against the justice of the capitalist system? Perhaps it would be, but the point (and others like it) is already covered by the criterion. It states that, "other things being equal," freedom of choice is a morally desirable feature of a system, as compared with a system that lacks this feature. Here, the system of conditioning does not count against the desirability of economic freedom—unless it could be shown that the existence of a system of propaganda has, as a necessary condition, the presence of economic freedom. And how could it? There have been many non-capitalist systems, lacking economic freedom, in which propaganda is present in abundance. Anyone even slightly familiar with the history of National Socialist Germany and Soviet Russia would find the linkage of propaganda with economic freedom unusual, to say the least. Perhaps one can counter that a particular sort of propaganda or conditioning depends on economic freedom for its existence: but, even assuming that such a speculative contention could be demonstrated, the charge seems much less damaging. If there is a particular kind of propaganda peculiar to capitalism, why is this important, given that there are other sorts of propaganda present in other systems? The only hope for someone interested in pursuing this objection would be to contend that a system of propaganda under capitalism is both inevitable and peculiarly nefarious. In the absence of a demonstration to this effect, the supporter of the Marcusean line can at best conclude that *if* capitalism does necessarily involve the use of propaganda or conditioning, and *if* a competing social system that he favors lacks this feature, that is a moral advantage of his system.

The criticism of the moral value of freedom, then, does not appear to be the most promising line of attack on the capitalist argument. A better try might lie in the contention that other systems than capitalism also have freedom of economic choice. Jon Elster, for example, places great emphasis on the wide measure of economic freedom persons living under market socialism enjoy in his advocacy of that system. In such a system, each firm is owned by those who work in it; there is no separate class of capitalists. The activities of the firms are coordinated by both government planning and the market. The role of each of these varies in different schemes of market socialism.[15]

If Elster is right, this once more says nothing against our argument. The argument does not claim that *only* capitalism is characterized by economic freedom, but that it is so characterized. If market socialism does indeed equal capitalism from the point of view of freedom of choice, then that issue cannot be raised in a comparison between these two systems. This leaves the argument for the justice of capitalism unscathed. Capitalism, along with any other system that possesses economic freedom, has *prima facie* a point in its favor.

But is Elster correct that persons living under market socialism enjoy the same, if not greater, economic freedom than those living in a capitalist system? It does not appear that he is right if one attends to the full force of the criterion. "Economic freedom" refers not only to the presence of a variety of consumer goods, but also to the freedom to enter into any economic transactions one is able to agree on with others. Included in what Nozick calls "capitalist acts between consenting adults"[16] are transactions involving production. In a market socialist system, workers produce most goods in cooperatives that they control and usually own as well, subject to central direction by the government planning board. But what if people do not wish to produce in cooperatives? What if, instead, they wish to labor for a private factory owner? As we shall see in a subsequent chapter, there are excellent reasons for thinking most people will *not* wish to work for cooperatives—for one thing, at least at certain wage levels, people tend to be risk-averse, unwilling to have their salaries dependent on the vagaries of profit and loss.

Regardless of the number of people who wish to work for cooperatives, however, can a market socialist regime permit dissidents to exit from the system? Assuming that the number of such people is at all substantial, it seems unlikely that it can. A regime in which workers and others exited from the system would soon cease to be a market socialist economy. The government of such a regime will then be faced with the choice of abandoning its chosen system or calling a halt to the workers' exodus. David Schweickart, a leading advocate of market socialism, admits that capitalist firms would have to be prohibited in the early stages of the system. He hopes that at a later time, the use of coercion could be relaxed.[17] A market socialist economy that defied Schweickart's prescription and allowed complete economic freedom might face the constant danger of dissolution. If it turned out that capitalist firms tended to be more efficient in production and attractive to workers than cooperatives, the cooperatives would soon exit from the scene. Also, there is the more direct point that in a market socialist order, the cooperatives stand subject to central direction by the government. A system without this feature would hardly qualify as socialist at all: it would either be entirely coordinated by the market, and thus be a variety of capitalism; have no coordinating mechanism at all, and thus reduce to chaos; or have some other type of coordinating control, of a hitherto unspecified type. The issue of cooperatives will be dealt with in much greater detail in Chapter 6.

Further, there is another aspect in which the argument that economic freedom exists in market socialism can be challenged: this issue will concern us several times in later discussion. On the criterion of justice we have suggested, economic freedom is a matter involving any and all people in a society able and willing to find others to make exchanges with them. It is not limited to a particular class of the population. More specifically, even if the workers form the great majority of the population, a regime that confines freedom of economic activity to them will not meet the requirements of our criterion. Marxists, even those of the analytical school, tend to ignore this point, as we shall later see. They tend to equate questions of freedom with the issue of what workers are at liberty to do, forgetting that there are other sorts of people besides workers.

Perhaps the market socialist can successfully counter this point by contending that, under his system, practically everyone will be a worker. It would not be a good reply to this counter to point out that some people do not wish to be workers but would, if free to do so, pursue other lines of endeavor. This, while true enough, is just the point against market socialism raised before. It does not address the issue we are now imagining the market socialist to raise: given that, willing or not, everyone in the society is a worker, it is irrelevant to point out that the issue of freedom is confined by the Marxist to workers.

But is this rejoinder in fact irrelevant? Given that everyone is a worker, there is indeed no group excluded by the society. But given the widespread opposition to the Marxist system on the part of large segments of the population, it seems unlikely that "everyone" would willingly be a worker. Rather, opponents of the regime seem liable to be subject to coercive penalties. Thus, our original point returns: Marxists *do* tend to concentrate all their attention on the workers when questions of economic freedom are raised, to the exclusion, at least, of opponents of the system.

To this, the market socialist might reply that the use of coercion, whatever the case in existing Marxist systems, does not play a role in his preferred plan. Further, isn't the appeal to historical evidence to support the contention that Marxist regimes deal more drastically with their opponents than just converting them to workers just the sort of historical appeal we have earlier criticized the Marxist for using?

To reply first with an *ad hominem* argument, it does not appear that Marxists can reply in the indicated way while remaining consistent with their system. It is a cardinal belief of Marxism that there will be considerable opposition, requiring forcible suppression, to the institution of a socialist system. "The history of all hitherto existing societies is the history of class struggle," as the *Communist Manifesto* famously proclaims. Following the overthrow of capitalism, a "dictatorship of the proletariat" will be established that will with "revolutionary terror" uproot the supporters of the old order.

To this the defender of market socialism might reply that *he* does not favor this picture of capitalism's overthrow. More plausibly, he might point out that it does not follow from the fact that classical Marxism imagines a social transition taking place in a certain way that if a socialist regime does replace capitalism, it will do so in the sanguine manner predicted by the Marxist founding fathers. Here, though, the classical Marxist position seems correct. Granted that the Marxist places primary emphasis on the institution of a particular economic system, and given the fact that many people oppose that system, violence is indeed liable to ensue when the system is established, lasting for the duration of such opposition. And the existence of opposition is not a mere inductive generalization. We have assumed that people value economic freedom: unless, then, they confine their preferences in this area to the bounds established by their Marxist rulers, or unless they see the system as so advantageous to themselves that it outweighs any disadvantages accruing from the lack of freedom, we can safely predict the existence of opposition. And that the opposition will find the regime to its liking is unlikely, since it is specifically aimed at the advantage of the proletariat and the establishment of socialism above all other goals, if not to their total exclusion.[18] If this line of reasoning is correct, the reply to the charge that Marxist regimes ignore non-workers fails. Such a regime does not change everyone into a worker; rather, it suppresses (or simply eliminates) the recalcitrant.

Whatever the deficiencies of market socialism, however, we are far from done with our criticisms of the argument for the justice of capitalism. First, the proponent of socialism may attempt to reverse the argument deployed here against his system. Just as we have discussed the possibility that workers and others will not wish to work in cooperatives, so may the opponent of capitalism raise the issues of those who do not wish to work for capitalists. What about those who prefer working for cooperatives? And what about those who wish to be employed by state enterprises? There are, after all, many people who actually prefer socialism, regardless of the defects opponents find in it.

No such reversal of the argument is valid, and a slight modification of the criterion suffices to take care of this issue. Although capitalism is characterized by private ownership of the means of production, those in a capitalist system who wish to form cooperatives are at perfect liberty to do so. (We shall examine G. A. Cohen's argument that this is not the case in Chapter 5.) Further, those who wish to set up "public" institutions are free to do so, provided they do not coerce others. If people wanted to have a large-scale health service which offered free treatment to the poor, they could agree to have contributions taken from their salaries to finance it. The agreement, further, could be a one-time-only affair, binding them in perpetuity.[19] In theory, a regime that started out as one of private ownership could transform itself into a system in which private ownership did not exist, and could do so by completely non-coercive means. And if it did, the advocate of the justice of capitalism would have nothing to say against it, no matter how much he might criticize the decisions of those in the system on grounds of efficiency.

It is therefore obvious how the criterion we have proposed must be modified. It is only necessary that one start with a system of private ownership: persons are, given their original entitlements, free to enter into any economic arrangements that they wish, regardless of whether these are conventionally denoted 'capitalist.' (Incidentally, the criterion says nothing about the justice of particular initial entitlements. This will be discussed in a later chapter.) Indeed, the modification of our criterion is not really an alteration: it simply makes explicit the extent to which freedom of economic activity is permitted to go.

It might be objected to this extension that, under it, any system counts as capitalist, provided it is established non-coercively. But then the extended definition does not adequately distinguish capitalism from other systems, but is at best a criterion of a non-coercive system. On the contrary, the criterion is still quite restrictive. Not only must one begin from a system of private ownership, as just mentioned; it also must be the case that people remain free to leave the non-private institutions they wish to establish. As will be shown in subsequent chapters, furthermore, it seems unlikely that many people in a system of private enterprise will find it rational to alter the private character of the system.

Another objection to the criterion does not have an exclusively Marxist provenance. According to the criterion, it will be recalled, two or more people can make any economic arrangement on which they mutually agree: the approval of third parties, however affected by the transaction, is not required. For example a seller might undersell his competitor, putting the latter out of business, without in any way seeking his approval or compensating him. It might be contended that this is too lax a standard: changes in an economy should not benefit anyone without compensation to those who are made worse off.[20] The issues raised by this objection are difficult; however, there is an easy way around them.

The problems posed by the third-party effects of economic transactions are not central to the debate between capitalism and socialism; an exception is that existence of certain types of wage bargains may adversely affect workers' solidarity (a matter we shall deal with in Chapter 5). Thus, it is not necessary to consider the vexed matter of externalities in detail here. Suffice it to say, first, that no society can with any likelihood exist if stringent Pareto-superiority is required for all changes: practically any change will make someone worse off, so the Pareto requirement threatens to produce stagnation. To put the matter in a simpler way, very few if any changes just help people, while making no one worse off. But this is exactly what Pareto-superiority requires. (See the discussion at note 20, and the source cited there.) It is also unclear why this standard is the right one: *why* must changes secure universal consent? Do people have the right to prevent any worsening of their position? Second, in the view of many economists externalities do not, even from the standpoint of welfare, pose a major challenge to the capitalist economy, although considerable difference of opinion exists on whether governmental intervention is required to take care of them.[21] Finally, even if economic freedom did have negative effects on welfare, this would again be a case in which the "other things being equal" clause of our criterion comes into operation. If capitalism led to negative effects on welfare while some other system did not, this fact would have to be balanced against whatever importance one accords to economic freedom. (Of course, this assumes the other system lacks economic freedom.) There seems little reason *a priori* to think that socialism handles this problem better than capitalism: why is a central planning agency likely to take into account the effects of its plan on those made worse off by it? True, it *can* consider them if it wishes—but why need it do so rather than attempt to realize its plans, objectors notwithstanding? But the exact settlement of these issues involves empirical analysis that we cannot undertake here.

II.

The argument for the justice of capitalism has so far withstood everything hurled against it. But all of what has gone before is prologue: we must now confront the main Marxist objection to the justice of capitalism. This is that the system of necessity rests on the exploitation of labor. We have pretended, the Marxist will say, that economic freedom is a matter of people agreeing to better their positions as they wish. Aside from difficult (but, in practice, relatively minor) issues such as externalities, how can one reasonably object to this? But, says the Marxist, this is just the surface; it is not in itself false, but it conceals the underlying reality of the system. Far from there being a system of equal bargainers, capitalism inevitably creates two classes: capitalists (owners of the means of production) and workers. The former, having brought it about that the latter have no choice but to work for them, extract profits through workers' exploitation. It is no use talking of free economic activity in the context of a system in which the wealth held by the members of each of the two main classes varies so greatly. "Freedom" in such an arrangement is but a sham: to talk of the justice of capitalism is to stand on empty verbiage.

Before confronting this argument head-on, three preliminary points need to be considered. These points are, in my view, valid; however, they do not in themselves suffice to overthrow the Marxist claim. First, we may remark on the incongruity of the use of "exploitation"—a term suggesting injustice—by Marxists, when Marx himself did not have a theory of justice. Quite the contrary, he scorned statements of rights as empty; from the point of view of his system of economic determinism, he was perfectly right to do so.[22] As mentioned in Chapter 1, this topic has generated much recent controversy; even those who do profess to locate favorable references to justice in Marx's work, however, have been hard-pressed to come up with a developed view of justice that can be attributed to him.[23]

But even if Marx was inconsistent in using the moral term "exploitation," this does not resolve the argument against him. Most people, after all, do use moral language; the assessment of the claim of exploitation does not require that one adopt Marx's own opinions on the role of morality. In fact, the analytical Marxists (especially Cohen and Elster) have been in the forefront of those attempting to develop a theory of justice compatible with Marxist conclusions.[24]

Second, the issue of class conflict arising through the split between capitalists and proletarians, the basis on which the theory of exploitation rests, cannot be adequately handled by distinguishing, in the manner mentioned above, between historical issues and theoretical ones. One might at first think that one *can* make use of this distinction. Just as the definition of capitalism we have presented does not require that the bad conditions of the Industrial Revolution (if one accepts, as I do not, the anti-capitalist portrayal of that event) are part of the system, so, it may be thought, the same applies to the division of classes. Indeed, the definition does not give any specification at all of the initial pattern of distribution considered just, except that the means of production be held privately. We may, if we like, start from a system of ownership like that advocated by Hillel Steiner, in which everyone begins by holding an equal share of all valuable assets.[25] Whatever one thinks of this system, the definition is certainly compatible with it. How, then, can it be the case that a capitalist system of organization *must* lead to a division into two classes? Has Marx confused a historical with a theoretical claim?

It is quite true that, as pointed out when the definition of capitalism was introduced, it does not follow from the concept of capitalism that a division into classes must result. But we left an escape for the Marxist in our previous discussion; he might attempt to show by argument, using premises additional to the definition, that capitalism does inevitably lead to the split in classes that the Marxist postulates. Exactly this path has been taken by John Roemer in his *General Theory of Exploitation and Class*. Briefly, he attempts to show that, on plausible assumptions, virtually any capitalist system will split into classes of exploiters and exploited. Unless absolute equality of resources is maintained throughout all later exchanges, even Steiner's system will develop classes. These classes need not correspond exactly to capitalists and workers, as assumed by Marx himself. The validity of Roemer's argument will not be challenged here: it is only essential now to see that if he is right, the thesis of class division is much more than a purely historical one. For the purposes of the present discussion, we shall assume that he is right. More exactly, without accepting or rejecting specific details of his theories, we shall endeavor to challenge the doctrine of exploitation on grounds other than the contention that its basis in class division is not inevitable.

Finally, a seemingly plausible line of attack on Marxist exploitation appeals to a fact discussed in the Introduction: the labor theory of value is generally held by economists, at least those outside the Soviet sphere, to be fallacious. But if the labor theory underlies the Marxist theory of exploitation, as it appears to do, doesn't the demise of that theory destroy the basis for charging capitalism with exploitation of workers?

The matter is not quite so simple. First, even if the labor theory is false, it might still be the case that capitalists exploit labor, as this term is used by Marxists. Suppose, for example, that economists come to consider some version of the subjective or marginal utility theory better than the labor theory. According to marginal utility theory, economic value is not an objective property of goods. Rather, economic value depends on the preferences of consumers.[26] It might still be the case that exploitation of labor in the Marxist sense takes place. That is, it might still be true that workers sell their labor power and receive in return enough to sustain their labor, and that the difference in value between what they produce and what they receive as wages is the source of rent, interest, and profit, even if it is not the case that the values of goods, including labor, are determined by the socially necessary labor time required to produce them. Second, John Roemer, in the book already mentioned, has developed a recognizably Marxist picture of exploitation that does not depend on the labor theory of value. Instead, in his view, the key to exploitation is that people hold assets of different values. Once again, we shall not assess the validity of Roemer's argument in this chapter; rather, we shall attempt to criticize the exploitation theory in a way that applies even if his theory is true. Finally, although the labor theory is indeed discredited, as we shall see at length in the next chapter, it is still interesting to inquire whether, if it were true, it would have the consequences that Marxists think it does. Nothing in the remainder of this chapter, then, will assume the falsity of the labor theory.

This, of course, does not mean that we accept the Marxist account of exploitation. The fundamental flaw of that doctrine is evident. "Exploitation," whatever the distaste that Marx had for the use of moral language, is clearly a moral term with a strongly negative connotation. Yet on the labor theory, all that it means is that, as already indicated, there is a discrepancy between the value the employer of labor secures by hiring a worker and the value the laborer receives back in payment. This has been stated in a rather general form, in order to illustrate the point made earlier that the charge of exploitation does not depend on the specific details of the labor theory of value. To reiterate, even if Marx's analysis of wage determination is wrong, it might still be the case that wages are less than the value workers contribute to their product.

But to return to our main argument against the exploitation theory, why should this difference between contribution and payment, if it exists, be considered morally bad? What is wrong with it? Is it supposed to be self-evident that the laborer is morally entitled to receive all of the economic value his labor adds to the product as judged by the labor theory? Surely some argument is owed us here.

Perhaps the argument is as follows: (1) Laborers should receive what they contribute to the value of the product. (2) If laborers receive only enough to produce (that is, support) themselves and to enable them to reproduce their number, then they are receiving less than their contribution to the product. (3) Therefore, workers under capitalism are exploited.

A course of attack on this argument that I find persuasive, but which is quite controversial, is to deny premise (1). This premise appears *prima facie* more plausible than the earlier claim that workers should receive the full economic value of what their labor power produces. It is precisely the value added by labor power less wages that accounts for all of the capitalist's profit, according to the labor theory. Faced with that claim, one may well reasonably inquire: why should workers be entitled to all of the profit, given that they use capital that does not belong to them? To reply that the capitalists unjustly hold their property as the result of past exploitation of labor is unsatisfactory. In addition to begging the question, this argument is irrelevant. It does not follow from the claim that capitalists hold their assets unjustly that workers employed by capitalists are entitled to the value produced with the aid of this capital. All that the claim states is that capitalists lack just title to their assets. But this does not show who, if anyone, ought to possess those assets. No capitalist can rightfully claim to own the planet Venus. It does not follow that workers should own it.

But faced with (1), is denial so easy a course to follow? Shouldn't workers receive what they contribute to the product they produce? I would claim, following the criterion for the justice of capitalism given at the beginning of this chapter, that persons should be free to enter into any arrangement they mutually agree upon. Thus, even if it is the case that workers receive less than they contribute to the product they produce, no case of injustice has been established.[27]

But, one might reply, if the capitalist does not pay the worker what he contributes, then the worker is at a disadvantage: surely this is a morally questionable state of affairs. Here, the key is "disadvantage": what does it mean? If it simply means that it is unjust that the worker receive less than he contributes, this begs the question: just the point we are considering is what makes this unjust, if indeed it is so. If, again, it means that workers would like to receive the full value of what they contribute, so what? It can hardly be a requirement of justice that each person in society receive what he would like to receive.

At this point, the defender of premise (1) may reply as follows. Workers are not at a disadvantage in any question-begging sense of the term. Rather, they are compelled to work for capitalists whether they wish to do so or not. They have no alternative. "Who does not work, neither shall he eat." As workers do not own capital goods, they must accept whatever terms the capitalist chooses to offer them.

In these imagined circumstances, workers would be at a disadvantage. I would once more maintain that, from the point of view of justice, nothing objectionable is involved here, unless capitalists do in fact use force or the threat of same to compel workers to serve them, or unless they have acquired their property unjustly. And in the latter case, the objection from justice applies to their obtaining property, not to what they subsequently do with it.

But this is a course that many people will be unwilling to take. Even those who reject the approach to justice favored here should recognize, however, that it is not entailed by labor's receiving less than the value it contributes to its product that any of the unfortunate circumstances just referred to obtain. Laborers need not, according to the concept of capitalism, be impoverished: they can be quite well off, even richer than the capitalist who employs them. It need not be the case that a laborer holds no assets or has no other alternative than to work for capitalists. Also, as far as work itself is concerned, every social system will necessitate that most people engage in labor, unless one assumes a state of complete abundance. Workers are free to form cooperatives, should they so desire. As we shall see in Chapter 5, G. A. Cohen questions this, but his argument is only that workers in existing capitalist systems will find it difficult to form cooperatives, not that the concept of capitalism logically entails their impossibility. And in this instance, neither Roemer nor anyone else has shown that capitalism must logically lead to impoverished workers.

Further, suppose workers are impoverished and do not have practical alternatives to working for a capitalist. Before going on, one should note that it does not follow that impoverished people have no alternative to working for capitalist employers. Many businesses require little in the way of assets except "human capital," which everyone possesses. These businesses include advertising and consulting firms, literary and other agencies, freelance writing, and so forth. It also does not follow that those who work for others will receive particularly bad terms. As long as there exists competition among employers, won't there be a tendency to bid wages up? The fact that a worker *would* accept a very low wage if he had no alternative to its acceptance except starvation does not imply that he will receive no offer any higher than that. What the wage rate in particular cases will, in fact, turn out to be is a matter best left to economic theory. We have only been endeavoring to show: first, that the existence of a discrepancy between labor's contribution to output and its reward does not imply the existence of poor conditions for labor; and second, that even if laborers were in fact impoverished, it does not follow that their employers could "take advantage" of them in a morally questionable sense. Of course, at this point the Marxist can appeal to other elements of his system that negate the assumption that competition exists among employers. He will no doubt say that collusion among capitalists sets up a "reserve army of the unemployed" that is used to cut down wages. This is not the place for an evaluation of that doctrine, but it can readily be seen that this notion is not entailed by the contention that workers receive less than what they contribute. What we wish to evaluate is the consequences of that assumption, not the consequences of assuming the truth of the entire body of Marxist economic theory.

Even if workers cannot be shown to be disadvantaged in a sense that is morally bad, given only the premise that they receive less in payment than they contribute in value, a nagging question remains. If they are not at a disadvantage, why the discrepancy? Further, even if there is no clearly establishable sense in which workers are at a disadvantage if premise (1) is rejected, many people will still find this state of affairs intuitively unacceptable.

If it turns out that, in a market economy, premise (1) is violated, it will of course be the task of economic theory to show why the situation obtains. That it is not due to workers' impoverishment is shown, in addition to the points raised previously, by the fact that the Marxist thinks the difference between labor power and the value of labor holds regardless of how high or low the position of workers is. Although the "reserve army of the unemployed," etc., is necessary to keep the capitalist system in existence, any employment of labor involves this discrepancy. Of course, however, the Marxist could be wrong about this: it could turn out that impoverishment is necessary for the discrepancy to exist. In that case, given that it is not necessary that workers be impoverished, the force of the "worker's disadvantage" argument would be blunted as a general indictment of capitalism. But we have given some reason above for thinking that any alleged worker disadvantage does not rest upon worker impoverishment.

So far, we have merely hinted at an absolutely fundamental point. Is it in fact the case that the market rejects premise (1)? Perhaps workers do in fact receive the value of what they contribute to their product: conventional non-Marxist economic theory assures us that, except in cases of a monopoly purchaser of labor, workers receive the discounted marginal value product of their labor. In other words, each worker receives the amount that the *last* or marginal worker adds to the value of the product. This is discounted by the rate of interest. But if this is so, then the Marxist question arises: how can the capitalist make a profit? (In Chapter 3, the suggestion that capitalists gain a profit through paying all workers only the value of the marginal product will be discussed.) Here profit is used not in the sense of entrepreneurial gain through superior economic judgment, but rather in the sense of a rate of return on invested capital. The answer to this is that labor receives, according to conventional theory, only the contribution directly imputable to it: it does not receive the full economic value of the product, since both land and capital, as well as labor, contribute to the value of the product. Although I cannot assert this with certainty, it may be that the Marxist claim that labor is denied its full contribution rests on the dubious position that labor is rightfully entitled to the full value of the product.

But, the Marxist may reply, unless there is the postulated discrepancy between the value of labor power and labor, how does profit arise? The question posed here is one of the most difficult in economic theory, and no answer to it will be attempted here. Rather, we wish only to question an assumption of the way this question is posed. The Marxist wishes to arrive at a mechanism by which profit is automatically generated in the capitalist system. But why must such a mechanism exist? Perhaps there is no general way in which a rate of return on investment is assured to the capitalist. In the view alluded to in the preceding paragraph, profit will arise whenever a capitalist succeeds in obtaining a greater price for his products than he has paid for the various factors of production that produce it. Profit, on this view, can arise from anywhere in the system, but it need not arise at all. Of course, the system could not work if no capitalists made profits. But from "If the capitalist system is to work, some capitalists must make profits," it does not follow that "There exists in the general case some mechanism for producing profit." Whether the view of profit briefly sketched above is correct is a question for economic theory to settle. But even if it is wrong, we can still see the questionable nature of the Marxist assumption that there must be a general mechanism for the production of profit.[28]

In the beginning of this part of the chapter, it was indicated that the falsity of the labor theory of value would not be assumed in arguing against the exploitation theory. To an extent, this promise has already been redeemed in our discussion of whether Marxist exploitation is morally bad, given its occurrence. In conclusion, two arguments will be suggested, neither of which involves a moral claim, aimed at showing that the presence of exploitation under capitalism in the technical sense of the term—the difference between the total value created by labor power and the value actually paid to labor (that is, the surplus value)—does not follow logically from the labor theory of value. For these arguments to hold, the labor theory must be taken strictly to state only that the value of a good is the average labor time socially necessary for its production. The entire body of Marxist economic theory must not be included in the theory.

First, from the labor theory of value, premise (2) of the argument given above to support the claim of exploitation does not follow. Unless workers' labor power does in fact add more to value than they receive in wages, no profit can be obtained. If it does not, and the Marxist view of the origin of profit is correct, the capitalist for whom labor power does not turn out to have a greater value than labor will make no profit. But, as we have already noted, it does not follow from the labor theory that there exists a mechanism that in the general case ensures that the value of the labor power exceeds the value of labor.

Finally, in Chapter 3 it will be argued that it does not follow from the labor theory of value that the capitalist is buying labor power while paying only for labor. It may well be (or so, at any rate, we shall claim) that workers are paid the full value of their labor power.

To sum up, a *prima facie* argument for the justice of capitalism has been presented. Several challenges to it, most notably one involving the Marxist doctrine of labor exploitation, have been analyzed. In the next chapter, we shall consider in detail how the analytical Marxists have modified, and rejected, crucial elements of classical Marxism.

3

The Analytical Marxist Rejection
of Classical Marxism

Analytical Marxists characteristically wish to do away with the labor theory of value. Further, they do not wish to replace Marx's labor theory with another labor theory of value—they reject theories of this sort altogether, or at least manage to do without them in their own work. Such a practice raises two questions which the present chapter addresses. First, on what grounds do they reject the labor theory of value? Second, can they reject the theory while remaining Marxists?

The second question may be expressed in a more pointed way. Marx used the labor theory to explain exploitation. Without it, on what basis can analytic Marxists claim that workers are exploited under capitalism? One can dismiss at once the possibility that they agree that the labor theory is needed to account for exploitation and hence do not believe that workers under capitalism are exploited. If they rejected exploitation, they would not be Marxists at all.

The analytic Marxists, fully aware of this difficulty, have responded by seizing the offensive. Not only is the labor theory unnecessary to explain exploitation; a better account is available. This new view of exploitation has principally been developed by John Roemer: it depends on differences of property holdings, not the discrepancy between labor power and labor cost, to explain exploitation. (It is not being claimed here that all analytic Marxists accept Roemer: rather, his approach is the most prominent one and has few rivals within the school.)[1]

Roemer's theory, as will be shown below, does not require Marx's labor theory to be false. Granted the belief of the analytic school, then, that Roemer's analysis of exploitation deepens the understanding of exploitation, the problem still arises: why abandon the labor theory of value?

In fact, the rejection of the labor theory proceeded independently from, and largely prior to, Roemer's work on exploitation. Two principal currents may be distinguished in the rejection of the labor theory: internal problems within Marxist economics, and difficulties with the argument advanced in the initial chapters of *Capital I* in support of the labor theory.

The internal problems were principally developed by Ian Steedman in *Marx After Sraffa*.[2] The view championed by Marx contends that the wages of labor are determined by the cost of producing the laborer: that is, wages are determined by the cost of the commodities the laborer needs in order to sustain his life according to the accepted social standard. Why? Because the value of labor power, like that of any other commodity, depends upon the labor required to produce it. Exploitation arises from the fact that the laborer has made available to the employer his labor power—his capacity to labor—which may exceed the labor cost required to produce it (that is, the cost of labor).

Steedman's principal criticism of Marx's account is a simple one. According to Marx's account, wages (and hence surplus value) depend on the commodities required to sustain the laborer. To simplify, imagine that laborers need only bread to survive. Then, according to Marx, wages depend on how much bread the workers require.

An ambiguity lies concealed in the phrase "how much." Does this mean how much in value terms, or in physical terms? That is to say, is the question at issue what quantity of bread the worker needs—or is it, rather, what the value of this quantity is? Marx took the question in the second way. The value of wages, in his view, depends on the value of bread the worker needs.

Steedman's objection is that once the physical quantity of bread at issue is given, this suffices to determine wages (and hence profits). The value of bread "drops out" of the picture altogether: no recourse to it is necessary in order to explain wages.

Steedman proves this through the presentation of a simple model, which he later complicates. At first, for example, he assumes that only one technique of production is necessary; later, he allows choice of technique. Although Steedman's argument does not require very difficult mathematics, I do not think I have a sufficient grip on it to try to explain his reasoning in detail. Rather, I shall attempt to present the basic point of his argument in my own way.

If wages depend on the value of bread, then we obviously need to know that value. But bread, like all other commodities, is subject to the labor theory of value, in Marx's view. To determine the value of bread, one needs to determine the value of the labor that produces bread. But the wages of bread-producers, like all other wages, depend on the value of labor power. This is turn depends on the value of bread, in the way earlier explained.

The circularity here is apparent. Before one can determine the value of labor power, one needs to know the value of bread, a value that in turn depends on the value of labor power. Unless one can break out of the circle, the labor theory's explanation of wages and profit fails.

Steedman himself favored substituting a theory advanced by Piero Sraffa in his *Production of Commodities By Means of Commodities*[3] for the standard Marxist labor theory. This system, like Marx's, relies on an objective measure of value, but uses a commodity other than labor as the unit of calculation (Sraffa's actual choice was "corn"—in American usage, grain). In Sraffa's system, labor's wage is not fixed by the cost of production of the goods needed to "produce" the laborer. Indeed, nothing within Sraffa's system fixes wages. They are an "exogenous variable" which, so far as the system is concerned, is arbitrary.

In Steedman's analysis of Marx, wage rates are indeed determined. However, this comes about only because Steedman assumes with Marx that the value of labor power depends on the bread needed by the laborer. Marx's argument for this depends on the part of the labor theory that Steedman has rejected: the *value* of labor power is determined by the *value* of the bread required to produce the laborer. Having rejected this, Steedman needs to provide another argument for the conclusion that wages are fixed by the physical quantities of goods required. He does show, if I am right, that *given* that wages are so determined, an explanation of wages and profits is available. But he does not argue that wages are fixed in this way.

Steedman's results place Marxists is a dilemma, should they wish to retain the standard Marxist account of exploitation. In

Marx's own view, there is a reason to assume a gap between the value of labor and the value of labor power, but Steedman had shown the inadequacy of this view. On the physical analysis that Steedman proffers to meet the problem he has raised for the standard Marxist account of wages, no reason is given to assume a gap between the wages and the value of what labor produces that suffices to explain profit.

Besides its main claim that, for reasons internal to the Marxist system, the labor theory ought to be abandoned, Steedman's work makes an additional point. In the course of his argument, Steedman contends that Marx's claim to explain profit by means of labor exploitation is merely a mathematical "trick."[4] (Steedman advances no claim that Marx was deliberately trying to "put one over" on his audience.) In any growing economy, total output will by definition exceed total costs. If costs and output are measured in labor-units, as they are by Marx, then total output in labor-units will necessarily exceed total costs in labor-units. But this comes about just because of the choice of the unit: if, as Bowles and Gintis picturesquely put the point, one used peanuts as the unit of measure, then total peanut-values would necessarily exceed total peanut costs in a growing economy. It would not follow that there is any quasi-magical power inherent in peanuts that enables capitalists to 'come out with' more value than they invest. Similarly, Marx's labor theory does not show that the purchase of labor is a 'special' sort of commodity. Marx has thus failed to explain the origin of profit through his labor theory.

As the point is rather unusual, perhaps a further example will help. The United States' Gross National Product is measured in dollars. If GNP increases, the new GNP consists of more dollars than the old. But it hardly follows that GNP has risen *because* the number of dollars has increased. The increase in dollars just *is* the measure of the GNP, not its explanation.

This argument, however, proceeds too quickly. It is certainly true that in an expanding economy, total output must by definition exceed total costs, whatever one's unit of measure. (A non-expanding economy raises no issue calling for discussion here, since in it there are no profits not balanced elsewhere by losses.) It does not follow from this, however, that Marx's account of profit fails. Rather, it could be (for all that the argument of the preceding paragraph has shown) that labor exploitation explains profit in exactly the way Marx assumes. If some other commodity than labor is selected as the unit of measure, then that commodity would not be a source of profit, even though profit was measured in its terms.

The case may be put in slightly different way. It is quite true that from the fact that in a growing economy the value of output (measured in labor) exceeds costs (measured in labor), the idea that labor produces the extra value does not follow. But the fact that output and costs are measured in a certain way does not exclude Marx's explanation of profit from being true. His argument for it does not depend on the mathematical 'trick' that Steedman and others have noted.

Another, more serious problem (one that is not addressed by Steedman) confronts Marx's account of wages and profits. According to the labor theory of value, a commodity's value depends on the labor necessary to produce it. But what is the value of labor itself?

This question cannot be answered. It is the equivalent of asking "How long is one foot?" or "How many miles in a mile?" Marx recognized this point. As he put it, labor is the substance of value: as such, it itself has no value.

A paradox then arises for the labor theory of value. Although the theory takes labor to be the basis of value, it seems that the price of labor cannot be explained by the theory.

Marx rejected this result. He claimed on the contrary that the paradox, if properly analyzed, solves the problem of how wages are determined.

The paradox stems from the assumption that the capitalist purchases labor. In fact, he doesn't. An employer obtains by his payment of wages a certain number of hours of labor from a particular laborer. It is as if the laborer were a machine whose services have been rented for a given period.

Understood in this way, wages can be determined without paradox by the labor theory of value. The employer purchases not labor but labor power—the capacity of a laborer to work. The value of labor power is the labor required to produce it, just as the value of a machine's services is the labor required to produce a machine capable of the services in question. Hence the paradox dissolves.

Marx's solution does not succeed. The value of a machine's services can be determined in the way Marx indicates just because the entire machine can be bought and sold on the market. The rent of a good, its services for a particular period, is a percentage of the good's total value. If Marx wishes to claim that the capacity to labor for a certain period is a commodity, then the total value of the laborer is also a commodity.

One can readily imagine circumstances in which laborers are bought and sold. In these circumstances, it would make sense to speak of renting labor. But the situation here is obviously a regime of slavery. In a capitalist economy, workers are not bought and sold. Neither, then, are they rented; and Marx's ingenious attempt to use labor power to explain wages fails.

A Marxist might be tempted to respond: "Isn't it obviously true that a worker *does* sell part of himself? In return for wages, the employer has 'bought' him for the hours he works." This response misses the point of the objection. The issue is not whether labor power is part of the laborer. Rather, the point in dispute is whether the value of labor power can be determined in a way analogous to the rent of a machine's services. To argue that it must be, since laborers do in fact receive wages, is to beg the question in favor of the labor theory. It does not follow from the fact that labor has a price that there must exist a satisfactory explanation of this price in terms of the labor theory of value.

Perhaps the point at issue can be made clearer in this way. Once someone has bought a machine, it is his to do with as he wishes. He can, if he wishes, devote the machine full-time to production. But workers are at liberty to decide how much of their labor services to offer on the market. No doubt workers must labor in order to survive; there is no reason, though, to assume they must offer for sale everything of which they are physically capable. How much labor they will offer depends crucially on wages. How, then, can the capacity to labor be taken to determine wages?

Unless, then, one assumes that the laborer is selling himself, the "classic" labor theory does not account for labor exploitation.

And if one does assume that the laborer is selling himself, one appears to have a case of exploitation from the start. (Normally, workers would not sell themselves rather than their labor power if they are free to do either.) The use of the labor theory to explain exploitation, then, either fails or begs the question.

Suppose, however, that Marx is correct. The value of labor power is the cost of production of the laborer. Does this, as Marx thought, expose the secret by which capitalists obtain profit? It does so only if the value of labor power is less than the value of what the laborer produces; otherwise, no surplus will exist.

But why should one assume that there is a gap between the value of labor and labor power? Of course, if wages cannot rise above subsistence, it is very plausible to think the gap exists—but, again, why assume this? If what workers need for their "production" may exceed a bare subsistence, as Marx himself allows when he notes that the rate of wages which will "produce" workers is socially determined, why won't wages rise until they equal the value labor adds to its product?

Marx might reply that various features of the capitalist system—for instance, employer collusion and the "reserve army of the unemployed"—operate to keep wages down. But then the gap between labor and labor power drops out of the explanation. What keeps wages down are just the features referred to. (I am, of course, not assuming that Marx is correct about either the existence of these features or of the gap.) Unless Marx can show that the features of capitalism that prevent workers from bidding up wages depend upon his labor power account, the latter serves no function.

The criticisms discussed so far have concentrated on Marx's account of profit. But even if this must be rejected, what about the labor theory in general? The analytical Marxists have not neglected this topic.

Jon Elster, in *Making Sense of Marx*, offers an especially critical account of Marx's derivation of the labor theory. Marx's argument may be put briefly as follows: one cannot explain why two commodities exchange in a given ratio by appeal to their use values (use value being, roughly, the use made of a good in consumption). These are incommensurable. If, for example, one loaf of bread can on the market be exchanged for two oranges, there is nothing in the use values of bread or oranges which will explain the ratio. Instead, one must abandon the concrete realm of use for a more abstract concept.[5]

In other words, as particular uses of goods will not explain their exchange rates, Marx sought the solution in an abstract unit to be found in any good, regardless of its use. This, he thought, could only be labor. Unless goods exchange according to the labor time necessary for their production, the exchange ratios of commodities could not be explained.

Elster objects that it has not been shown that only labor can "fill the bill" of being the factor underlying an exchange ratio. Why not, for example, energy?[6] Marx gives no argument that one must use labor—indeed, he does not consider other alternatives. Further, Marx contends that it is not just any labor that can be used in explaining exchanges. The labor must be "socially necessary"—that is, it must not be the case that more labor is employed to make a particular product than the "standard" amount needed to produce a commodity under given social conditions. One can readily see the reason Marx advanced this qualification. Without it, an inefficient laborer who took a great deal more time than average to produce something would be counted as producing more valuable goods than an efficient worker.

But with the introduction of "socially necessary" labor, a new problem arises. How does one determine what the socially necessary labor for a given commodity is? It seems difficult to do so without resorting to prices (that is, exchange ratios). But it is just these ratios that the labor theory endeavors to explain. It looks reasonable to say, then, that the labor theory explains exchange rates only by first assuming their existence. The theory appears to be guilty of arguing in a circle.[7]

These difficulties (and other ones) that Elster mentions need not be rehearsed at length. His comments, on the whole, reproduce a fairly standard list; they do not advance the subject beyond the classic analysis of Böhm-Bawerk.[8] A more original difficulty for the theory emerges from recent work by G. A. Cohen. Cohen, it should be noted, intends his remarks as a clarification of the labor theory, rather than an argument against it; they may nevertheless, however, be used for this purpose.[9]

Cohen notes an ambiguity in the usual statement of the theory. Is the value of a commodity the socially necessary labor that has gone into its production? Or is it, instead, the socially necessary labor that would be required if this item were now to be produced? At first sight, one might incline at once to adhere to the former alternative: this, in fact, is how the theory is almost always presented. But why does some past fact explain the value of a commodity that exists now? Is not the relevant fact something about its present qualities? The labor that has gone into the making of a good is past and gone. How, then, can it determine value? Cohen accordingly adopts the second alternative, citing textual evidence that Marx saw the matter in his way.

Cohen now lays himself open to an objection which has been made by Jan Narveson.[10] The labor that would be required to produce a good, in contrast with the labor that has made something, is a hypothetical magnitude. "What would be" is, by definition, not now existent. How, then, can it explain the value of something? Surely only an existing magnitude can explain a present value.[11]

Cohen could readily respond to this point. (So far as the writer is aware, he has not in fact considered this issue in print.) It is no doubt right that a hypothetical cannot cause a good to have value by itself: but it can if economic actors have this magnitude "in mind" and their using it enables their valuations to be explained. But if Cohen has so easy an escape available, why was it said above that his work raises a difficulty for the labor theory?

The answer lies exactly in the proposed escape from Narveson's objection. If labor value needs to "pass through" the minds of economic actors in order to take effect, does this not tend to show that value is not the objective phenomenon that Marx assumed it was?[12] On the "hypothetical" interpretation of the labor theory, value operates through the minds of the economic actors, who consider the hypothctical labor valuation in their decisions. Were they to fail to do so, then Narveson's criticism would return: a hypothetical, by itself, can cause nothing.

This point, however, does not overthrow the classic labor theory. It is not clear that the labor theory is bound to the hypothetical alternative, as opposed to the "standard" view. On the latter, once more, it is the labor that *has* been expended on a commodity that determines its value. In appealing to the inability of a past fact to explain a present value, Cohen has at most made a suggestive point. He has not shown any logical contradiction in the standard view. His comment has been mentioned, however, not because it succeeds in overthrowing the received view of the labor theory but because, to the extent one finds Cohen's point plausible, an altogether different approach to economic value comes into the range of vision.

The view in question is one that challenges Marx's argument at its first step: this is the subjective theory of value, which, as will shortly become apparent, has implications inimical to the entire Marxist system. It is discussed here not for its own sake—that is, as a matter of economic theory—but rather to show that if one pushes against the labor theory harder than the analytical Marxists have done, much more radical changes for Marxism ensue than those they contemplate.

A good place to begin is with a return to Elster's criticism. While he rightly challenges Marx's assumption that the constant factor underlying an exchange ratio must be labor, he leaves standing the view that an exchange is an equality. If, for example, one loaf of bread exchanges for one orange, why should one say that one loaf of bread *equals* one orange? It is not obvious, at any rate, that a relation of equality follows from an exchange.

On the Austrian theory of value—a view developed by Menger, Böhm-Bawerk, Mises, and Hayek—an exchange entails not an equality but a double inequality.[13] The person who acquires the orange will not make the trade unless he values the orange he acquires more than the loaf of bread he surrenders; likewise, the person who acquires the loaf of bread rates it higher than the orange he gives up. Members of the Austrian school contend that given these two inequalities, economic value (whether of production or consumption goods) can be explained. No resort to an "objective" magnitude is needed.

Although I find this view persuasive, one must in fairness note that not all authorities accept the "double inequality" contention. Robert Nozick, for example, in a characteristically intricate note in *Anarchy, State, and Utopia,* contends that it does make sense to say that one loaf of bread equals one orange, if the rate of exchange between bread and oranges is one loaf of bread for one orange. (His point has been adapted to the example given above.) His reasoning, very briefly, is that if one has a loaf of bread, one can secure one orange, barring transaction costs: hence the equality, for practical purposes, of the two. Given the exchange ratio, if you have one, you in effect have the other.[14]

However one may assess this point, it leaves untouched the criticism of the labor theory here being urged. Marx's argument assumes (as Nozick's does not) that exchange involves an equation—that is, an identity. If, in the example, one loaf of bread equals one orange, then Marx assumes that the expressions "loaf of bread" and "orange" are alternate names for the same "stuff." He then, of course, goes on to seek the nature of this "stuff," finding it in abstract labor.

It is worthwhile to pause a moment to see how radical Marx's assumption is. In an ordinary equation—say, $X + 3 = 12$—the sides of the equation both are different expressions for the same number (in this case, 9). The equation is really another way of saying "$9 = 9$." A market exchange certainly does not *seem* like an identity. Even if one rejects the "double inequality" view of exchange, why should one think that an identity underlies the items being traded?

Had this point been pressed by the analytic Marxists, they would have to face a challenge to their version of Marxism. If the Marxist account of objective value is eliminated as resting on the unproved and implausible position that an exchange is a strict identity, what follows?

Although this move is not logically necessary, one seems pushed in the direction of the subjective theory of value.[15] And it is here that the challenge to the analytic Marxist position looms. The most developed version of a subjective theory of value is that found in "mainstream" economics: for present purposes, the differences between various approaches to subjective value (for example, between the Austrian and neo-classical approaches) are not relevant. According to these theories, all factors of production receive their marginal value product. In other words, each factor gets what the last unit of that factor contributes to the value of production. (Actually, factors receive the marginal value product discounted by the rate of interest, but this does not affect our discussion.) If this is so (and although the theory will not be derived here, it follows uncontroversially from the "standard" subjective theory of value), then labor receives what it contributes to production. In short, not only is it the case that, as earlier contended, the labor theory gives us no grounds for saying that labor is exploited; furthermore, on the most developed alternative theory (which avoids the apparent fallacy that an exchange is an identity), exploitation has been disproved. "The laborer is worthy of his hire"; he receives just what his labor adds to the process of production.

The peril to analytic Marxism becomes evident at once. A "Marxism" that rejects the standard view of exploitation arguably can survive with another explanation of exploitation (for instance, Roemer's view, which is discussed below). But if the existence of exploitation is denied altogether, Marxism plainly has been abandoned.

Considering the significance of the marginal productivity theory, the analytic Marxists have not devoted very much attention to it. In particular, they have not addressed the contention that economic value is a subjective phenomenon. An objection to the contention that the marginal productivity theory precludes labor exploitation, however, has been raised by Elster.[16]

He notes that according to the theory, each worker receives the marginal product of labor in wages. But why, he inquires, should each worker receive only the marginal product—that is, the value contributed by the last worker? Elster's point is this: each worker except the last adds more than the product of the last worker to value. (We assume constantly diminishing marginal returns to simplify the example.) Why does the employer not pay each worker what he contributes to the product? Instead, the employer keeps the surplus that results from paying each of his workers what the least productive worker earns. The employer might reply that the difference in workers' products does not stem from differing skills: their wages should therefore be the same. This response is inadequate. Why not pay each worker the average product rather than the marginal product of labor?

If, however, a significant gap arises between average and marginal product, it will pay workers to form coalitions to prevent the employer from acting in the way Elster indicates. So long as the employer makes *some* profit, it will pay him to hire workers even if they largely succeed in closing the gap between marginal and average product. Only if the gap is less than the costs of forming a coalition will Elster's point assume importance in wage determination.

Unfortunately for this analysis, further complications arise. What if there are coalitions of employers or rival coalitions of workers? These issues will not be pursued here: until they have been resolved, it is difficult to say how much of a point Elster has.

Before turning to another objection to the marginal productivity theory, one caveat is in order. The theory is not part of ethics: it does not claim that the various factors of production ought to be paid their marginal value product. Some economists, most famously John Bates Clark, have advocated the ethical desirability of the theory's type of distribution. Others (for example, Frank Knight) have opposed it as an ethical system.[17] But its use here is descriptive; if it is a correct or near-correct theory of wage-determination under capitalism, then workers are not exploited in the standard Marxist fashion. They do not contribute more than they are paid.

An attack on this conclusion has been advanced by David Schweickart in his book *Capitalism or Worker Control?*[18] Although Schweickart is not usually listed as an analytic Marxist, he is an analytically trained philosopher interested in Marxism. His objection is discussed here because of the paucity of treatments of marginal productivity theory among the analytic Marxists.

Schweickart argues that, in contrast to labor, which performs a real productive function, capital itself produces nothing. The capitalist, as owner, merely allows production to take place by permitting workers to use his capital. His organizational activities are, according to Schweickart, part of "wages of management." In his strict function as a capitalist, he contributes nothing.

The force of Schweickart's response to marginal productivity theory is the following. He accepts that theory's account of how factor incomes are derived. He denies, however, that this account entails that labor is unexploited, since he believes that the entire share that goes to capital is its "reward" for doing nothing productive.

His criticism is not that capitalists do not ethically deserve to hold their assets, or that they have acquired them through a process that, at least at some stage, involves injustice. He believes these things as well, but his present criticism is different. It is that, regardless of whether the capitalist "deserves" his property, he makes no "productive" contribution. Hence, marginal productivity theory is undermined.

On a closer look, however, Schweickart's objection collapses at once. Capital is not a free good: only a certain amount of means of production are available in a given economy. Some person or group must then decide which products will be made. If so, then capitalists, in allowing their capital to be used in production, *are* performing a productive function. They are deciding which of the many goods that can be produced will be produced. This is a productive function because those decisions must, if profit is to be gained, lead to products that consumers wish to purchase. To direct production into channels desired by consumers—and, as a result, to gain profit—is an activity paradigmatically use*ful*.

One of Schweickart's arguments to the contrary in effect admits the point in dispute. He notes that it is not necessary that capitalists supply capital: economies are conceivable in which workers, organized in cooperatives, act as providers of capital. Other economies, not only conceivable but actual, allot this function to centralized planning boards.

No doubt Schweickart is correct. But the fact that, in non-capitalist economies, groups other than capitalists supply capital hardly shows that under capitalism, capitalists fail to exercise a productive function. Schweickart's claim in fact depends on the very assumption he denies. If, as he thinks, capitalists do not have to allocate resources to production because there are other ways of doing this, then there *is* a productive function that some people, capitalists or not, must exercise. If *someone* has to allocate resources, then are not capitalists productive when they do this? Further, the relevant question for the analysis of capitalism is what takes place in that system, not what occurs in alternative systems. One suspects that Schweickart's "real" point is that capitalists' possessions are unjust, in spite of his protestation that his objection is value-free. Whether or not this conjecture is right, however, Schweickart has left marginal productivity theory undamaged.

To sum up so far, the analytical Marxists tend to reject the labor theory of value. There seems to be good reason for them to do so, since the theory rests upon the odd assumption that an exchange is an equation—that is, an identity. Even if one accepts the labor theory, however, no rationale exists in it for the standard Marxist contention that workers are exploited under capitalism. And if one rejects the labor theory, one is faced with the fact that the main theory opposed to the labor theory, the marginal productivity theory of "mainstream" non-Marxist economics, seems to show that the laborer is not exploited.

What, then, is the analytical Marxist to do? If exploitation goes, then Marxism appears finished. Marxism without exploitation would be only a hollow shell of its former self. The analytical school has not taken this situation lying down. Particularly in the work of John Roemer, it has launched a strong counter-attack designed to show that the capitalist system *does* produce exploitation. If his views are right, he has undercut the arguments against exploitation which are based on marginal productivity theory. He redefines exploitation so that, even if marginal productivity theory is accepted, capitalism still leads to exploitation.

Roemer is a leading specialist in mathematical economics, and much of the detailed presentation of his work is rigorously technical. Fortunately, the notion behind his theory of exploitation is a simple one. He maintains that conventional Marxism errs in seeing the practice of laboring for capitalists as the cause of exploitation. The true cause of exploitation lies elsewhere, in different initial endowments of property.[19] Roemer shows mathematically, by a series of gradually more complicated examples, that if one starts with people owning different amounts of property, then a class structure will emerge. That is, given the differential endowments of property, some people will end up working for others.

We are not concerned here with the details of Roemer's various derivations. Many of his results, if correct, are startling: he argues, for example, that in certain plausible conditions, a system of differential ownership *must* lead to a five-class system.[20] But the fact that Roemer has derived such detailed conclusions with apparent rigor from the seemingly innocuous assumption of differential ownership of property should not prevent one from raising critical questions. Mathematical theorems, however rigorously derived, need to be interpreted if the structures they establish are to be applied to the real world of the economy. And this task cannot be accomplished by more mathematics.

If one attempts to interpret Roemer's results, his theorems appear much more different from Marx's account of exploitation than one might at first suspect. He does show that assuming different initial property endowments, some people will end up working for others. But he does not attempt to show a relation between this result and standard Marxist exploitation.

Here, I intend no criticism of Roemer. Rather, the point is that neither differential property ownership nor working for others has anything to do with standard Marxist exploitation. The latter arises because workers are alleged to receive less in wages than they contribute to output. The fact that some find it economically rational to work for others does not imply that they fail to receive the full value of what they produce. Neither does the fact that some people have to work longer than others imply that less than full value is received.

Nor does Roemer contend otherwise. Rather, his reason for labeling the situation exploitative is that although each person finds either working for an employer or employing workers advantageous, the employer has an 'extra' advantage. He can gain benefits without labor, just because (by Roemer's demonstration) it will be to the advantage of others to work for him. He is, in Roemer's view, essentially parasitic on the labor of others. He gains his consumption bundle with the exertion of less effort than they do.

In attempting to assess Roemer's exploitation doctrine, some further facts about Roemer's system are useful. Not only is there no requirement for a gap between labor output and wages in Roemerian exploitation; there is no necessity that workers receive a "low" standard of payment. Marx assumed that, although wage rates were determined in part by what a particular society viewed as an acceptable standard of living, workers under capitalism are in general quite badly off.[21] Roemer does not assume this: his "workers" can be quite wealthy and still be considered exploited, so long as they find it rational to work for others and others get their consumption bundles with less effort.

Further, on Roemer's assumption, it is possible for workers to exploit capitalists. Under some conditions, workers will find it profitable to hire capital rather than the reverse situation. In this case, as Roemer fully recognizes, his style of exploitation is present.[22] Further, exploitation is also possible in a socialist system, so long as some people have superior skills or status which they can use to secure higher-than-average incomes.[23] At first, to say that exploitation is present here appears paradoxical. How could workers exploit the suppliers of capital if the capitalists do not work under the workers? Roemer's answer is that the workers in the cases he believes are exploitative earn the same income with less effort than the capitalists. In like fashion, the superior socialist workers get more goods than the less-favored, but for just the same effort. In Roemer's view, if you "do better" than someone else, your advantage is the result of exploitation, so long as the initial distribution of assets is unequal. You do not have to employ someone to exploit him. One might, given these discrepancies from classical Marxist exploitation, expect Roemer to reconcile his view with the standard one in some way.

But he doesn't—in fact, he extends his definition of exploitation so that any group that would be better off if initial property endowments were equally distributed counts as exploited.[24] For example, if workers are doing extremely well economically but would have done even better if property had been equally distributed originally, they are now exploited. Very roughly, Roemer's concept of exploitation amounts to this: if people start off with unequal amounts of property or skills, the better-endowed will not have to work as hard as the worse-endowed to gain the same bundle of goods.

Here a problem raised for Marx's view of exploitation recurs in a much more obvious way. Just as one can ask "What is wrong with the exploitation of labor, as Marx conceives it?", a parallel query arises here. What is wrong with Roemerian exploitation? Why *shouldn't* people who are originally endowed with unequal assets gain an advantage in this way? Roemer might reply that, regardless of one's theory of justice, it seems evident that people who perform exactly the same labor should receive the same reward. If A and B do work identical in all respects, why should they be paid differently? Equivalently, if A's work is identical with B's but A works less than B, shouldn't he receive less? To deny this is, it seems, to sanction arbitrary discrimination. The argument, in this view, does not assume that equality is morally required. Rather, it contends that certain inequalities lead to results that almost everyone will condemn.

But Roemer has not shown that this state of affairs obtains. A and B are not identical in all respects if one of them starts out with more assets than the other. If A receives the same money for less effort than B, but also has greater initial assets, why should one say that A receives more money for the identical work than B? Why not say instead that they are paid identically, but that A receives extra income from his greater initial endowment?

Roemer needs to show that all of A's extra income should be imputed to his labor in order to make good his claim that possession of superior assets permits one to receive higher returns for identical labor. If Roemer does not do this, the question arises: what is wrong with Roemer's exploitation? All he has shown is that people who are originally endowed with unequal assets gain an advantage in the way indicated.

The question just suggested differs from another that also arises. What is wrong with initial inequality of resources? This question, which will be addressed in Chapter 4, clearly speaks to an important and controversial issue. Even if one finds egalitarian considerations of little or no force, the issue at least warrants discussion.

Once this question has been answered, however, it is difficult to see that Roemerian exploitation raises any issue at all worth considering. Whether or not initial inequality is morally "all right," what new issue arises? If initial inequality is morally "all right," nothing seems problematic about the fact that the better-endowed have the advantages to which Roemer calls attention. If initial inequality is not morally acceptable, then *this*—rather than Roemerian exploitation—is bad. Both egalitarians and their opponents ought to agree with the two preceding sentences. In sum, there is not even a *prima facie* case to be met that Roemerian exploitation is morally problematic. All it amounts to is the commonplace that better initially-endowed people are at an advantage.

In this respect, Roemer's argument is much inferior to Marx's. Marx's argument that workers are exploited because they sell their labor power but are paid only for the cost of labor can indeed be challenged in the same way as Roemer's claim. Why is Marxist exploitation bad? The difference between Marx and Roemer is that Marx does have a *prima facie* case requiring response. On his analysis, it *does* at first glance appear that the employer receives free hours of labor time from workers. This appearance, I have tried to show, dissolves upon closer examination. But Roemer's exploitation presents no case at all. Workers do not surrender free hours to anyone in his construal of exploitation; instead, some people earn more than others because of initial inequality. Inequality needs to be addressed directly, rather than renamed exploitation.

4

Analytical Marxism Versus Libertarian Rights

It was argued in Chapter Two that, other things being equal, a system in which people are free to make the exchanges they wish ranks as better than one without this feature. To be more specific, laissez-faire capitalism has just this desirable feature while socialism, as usually interpreted, does not. The very nature of socialism mandates that production and exchange occur within the limits set by a central plan. Some socialist systems allow much more free exchange than others, but none totally eschews central direction of people. Indeed, a socialist system that did so would transform itself into a different system. Without any central direction, what remains of socialism?

One might object to the argument in this way. No doubt under socialism individuals cannot in their economic life act as they wish, should their desires deviate from the plan. But every workable economic system requires for its operation that those living under it obey certain rules. Just as those living in a socialist society must obey the plan, so must individuals in a capitalist economy refrain from violating the property rights of others. One is not, under capitalism, at liberty to do whatever one pleases. In particular, those who possess little or no property may find that their freedom to make exchanges amounts to very little of benefit to them.

Any social system requires a principle of distribution of property and income. Once a society adopts a rule of distribution, those living in that society cannot, on pain of contradiction, be allowed to flout its terms freely. To allow people to make a rule more honored in the breach than in the observance of their society's method of distribution is senseless. If the principle of property distribution cannot be enforced, then the alleged rule is not in effect in practice. And not to have a distributive system at all stands as the very quintessence of chaos.

Socialism, like its capitalist rival, must possess a distributive rule. But once given the initial distribution of property, the systems at once diverge. So long as they do not use force or violence, those living under capitalism may do as they wish. (This of course overstates the case, but complications do not affect our discussion here.) Under socialism, a far different situation ensues. People cannot do whatever they wish (barring use of force or violence) with the property assigned to them. They face further restrictions in order that their activities conform to the dictates of the planners. They find themselves especially subject to strict bounds in the use of their resources for production.

Nor will it do to counter that these restrictions form part of the distributive rules: this being so, people—so long as they follow the rules of distribution—remain as free as under capitalism to use their resources as they wish. In response, one need only restate the point at issue with a slight variation. Under capitalism, but not under socialism, the rules of property distribution assign physical objects to owners and do nothing else. If you have justly acquired some parcel of land X, for example, you may use it, sell it, or let it lie idle, as you alone may think best.

A much better criticism of the argument for capitalism based on freedom of exchange is the following. True, people under capitalism can do things with their property that are forbidden to owners of property in a socialist commonwealth. But how do people under laissez-faire capitalism obtain their property? If they have done so unjustly, the liberty argument is crucially weakened. A robber who, after his initial depredations, allowed full freedom of exchange would not generally be taken to have established a desirable economic system. The argument that capitalist property rights are unjust is the principal topic of this chapter. Specifically, it will examine the strongest version of this argument—offered, as one might expect, by G. A. Cohen.

Cohen's argument begins by considering the initial appropriation of unowned property, which underlies all later acquisition. Before one can validly get property by trade, gift, or inheritance, someone must first have just title to it. Cohen subjects to close examination the libertarian arguments advanced by Robert Nozick in *Anarchy, State, and Utopia* and finds them lacking.[1] If

Cohen is right, the freedom found in capitalism rests on no foundation of justice. In the present chapter, we shall examine Cohen's case. Also, though much more briefly, we shall try to show that a weakness in that case is also fatal to the treatment of exploitation by John Roemer.

Nozick's theory of initial property acquisition places its author within the Lockean tradition. People acquire unowned property by "doing something" to it, so long as they observe the Lockean proviso. This requires that someone's acquisition of property not worsen the position of anyone else, taking the "state of nature" as a baseline.[2]

As is apparent even from this very rough sketch, Nozick is not a strict Lockean. He does not require, as Locke did, that people mix their labor with unowned property in order to take it into their private sphere. In fact, he raises arguments against labor mixture.[3] In place of what he regards as Locke's flawed principle, Nozick substitutes nothing at all. He confines himself to indicating that the task of a correct theory of initial acquisition is to arrive at a rule that withstands objections.

If Nozick wishes in this instance to let discretion be the better part of valor, this is his affair. While he should not be faulted for choosing to leave certain issues in his theory unsettled, the gap in his theory at once raises a question about Cohen's argument. Even if Cohen succeeds in undermining Nozick, he will be striking against a theory that, by its own lights, stands incomplete. It hardly counts as a decisive point against the justice of capitalism that an incomplete theory fails fully to convince.

The situation seems even worse for Cohen. A number of writers have developed Lockean theories of property acquisition that *do* specify a rule for initial acquisition. Among these are Murray Rothbard, Eric Mack, Douglas Rasmussen and Douglas Den Uyl, and Ellen Paul.[4] By confining his argument to Nozick, Cohen makes his case easier for himself than it should be. In particular, Cohen concentrates much of his fire on Nozick's Lockean proviso. But the writers just mentioned do not include this proviso; to a great extent, Cohen's assault passes them by.

Fortunately for Cohen, things are not quite so bad as this. Some of his arguments apply to most or all libertarian property theories.

One such point, on which Cohen places great stress, is the following: Nozick's theory (and many like it) assumes that property is initially unowned. But how do we know this? Why should we assume that property lies open to acquisition by individuals? Suppose, on the contrary, that the members of a society have collective rights to the territory they inhabit. They do not gain these rights by acting upon previously unowned property. On the contrary, the citizens of that society secure these property rights at birth, just as they do their civil liberties. If so, Nozick's theory has no room in which it can take hold. In the society we have conjured up, there is no unowned property to be acquired—by labor mixture or anything else.[5]

This contention is more radical than it first appears. Given a system of individual property rights, it is easy to understand how individuals can acquire shares at birth. But these shares exist only after a property system has been established. In a system of this kind, one starts with property initially unowned. People may, under certain conditions, acquire property and pass it on. Cohen is suggesting that systems allowing individual property rights wrongly take for granted the first step. He asks, why should one assume that property is *ever* initially unowned?

Cohen believes that this point undermines a seeming strength of the libertarian view, in that it blocks a direct derivation of individual property rights based on an intuitively plausible principle to which libertarians appeal. Advocates of that position place great emphasis on self-ownership (though some avoid this term). Each person has rights over his or her body on which others may not impinge. In the novelist Ayn Rand's memorable case, someone may not detach one of your corneas even to enable a blind person to see. Even if particular intrusions on self-ownership increase "social welfare," they are properly forbidden. (I have used scare quotes, since some advocates of this view question whether social welfare means anything.)

Cohen finds much intuitive force in the principle of self-ownership, and it is here that one grasps what lies behind his challenge to the assumption of unowned property. If people own themselves, why may they not acquire resources, so long as their doing so does not interfere with the self-ownership rights of other people? To stop people from acting in this way seems *prima facie* to count as just the sort of interference with individuals' freedom of action which self-ownership forbids. The case seems all the stronger when one adds that physical resources are needed for survival. How can someone who owns himself, and who does not interfere with others, be justly prevented from acting in a fashion essential to his well-being?

Cohen challenges this argument on the ground that self-ownership cannot be used to justify the acquisition of unowned property—at least not without adding a further premise. This extra premise is that (some) property is initially unowned. It doesn't follow just from self-ownership, that is, that the acquisition of unowned property can be justified. Cohen is correct that self-ownership does not entail that property in a society is initially unowned. More strongly, from the principle that each person owns his or her own body, nothing at all immediately follows about the ownership of other physical objects. But, of course, one cannot conclude from this that the assumption that property is initially unowned lacks substance.

What, after all, is the purpose of a theory of property? Unless one adopts the suicidal rule that no one may legitimately use any physical resources, one's theory must in some way "connect up" people with physical objects. Apart from the connections one's theory arrives at, physical objects are ownerless. They have no intrinsic connections with individuals or groups. Persons may carve their initials on trees; unless they do so, the trees will not have their names on them. It is in this (I hope) uncontroversial sense that one cannot, against Cohen, challenge the principle that property is initially unowned. What this principle means is that ownership stands in need of justification.

Cohen's own views do not avoid this sense of the principle. If people have collective rights over the territory that they inhabit, how did they acquire such rights? Cohen would need to confront this question if he in fact wished to develop a view along these lines.[6] Unless he does deal with it, the libertarian can respond to Cohen by saying that the *only* sense in which people can acquire property at birth is within an existing system of property rights which allows such a practice. If this is what acquiring property at birth means, then Cohen, in talking about it, has altogether evaded the question of how property is acquired. This kind of birthright can arise only after the principle of acquisition has been settled. If Cohen denies that he has shifted the issue from acquisition, then he needs to spell out how the rights he has in mind are justified.

Contrary to Cohen, then, the libertarian does not beg the question by assuming without argument that collective property rights do not exist. All that is assumed is that collective rights, like any other property rights, require support. Certainly, if collective property rights left no scope for individual acquisition of property, a libertarian view could not get off the ground. But this counts for nothing, so long as no defense of collective rights is in the offing.

One might object to this argument and say that it misconstrues the point at issue. Granted that any theory of property rights requires argument, it does not follow that one must assume that people exist before property. That is, one need not assume that a valid theory of property has this form: at some time, individuals exist without property who then engage in various activities in order to acquire it. It is indeed true that if one took this view for granted, one would beg the question against theories of collective rights of the sort Cohen favors.

But the Lockean theory does not make this false move. It tells us that *if* there is unowned property, it can be appropriated. It does *not* say that any unowned property lies available. Instead, the theory need only assume that in the absence of argument that property *is* owned, it should be taken as unowned. The burden of proof rests on whoever claims ownership.

The argument just given adheres to the spirit, if not the letter, of Nozick's text. In fact, Nozick denies that his theory bars ownership of property by groups. Collectives, as well as individuals, may acquire unowned property.[7]

Cohen pounces on a minor point here, but he ignores something important. He rightly notes that Nozick speaks of groups coming to acquire property. The passage cannot then, he thinks, be intended to address Cohen's problem: Nozick, as Cohen has contended all along, has taken for granted that property begins as unowned. Since Nozick speaks of *coming to* acquire property, is he not assuming that property was once unowned? This is just the point Cohen challenges. But one has only to modify Nozick's statement in order to handle Cohen's objection. All that is needed is to drop the phrase "coming to." Nozick will then be asking: "How do groups acquire property rights?" The Lockean theory stands acquitted of bias against collective ownership since it allows collective acquisition, and at the same time insists that all claims to ownership, whether individual or collective, require justification. By failing to juxtapose the passage he cites with the common-sense principle that any claim of ownership needs support, Cohen mistakenly concludes that Nozick's theory begs the question.

I have contended that a Lockean theory need not take for granted that people exist before property. The stronger position—that is, that people must do something to acquire property—seems intuitively plausible. Cohen himself may be assuming it at another place in his polemic, when he criticizes an argument of Nozick's against redistribution of wealth. Nozick, in the course of his argument against government redistribution, states on one occasion that property comes with claims of ownership attached: it does not drop from the heavens like manna. Here, Nozick refers to property of a sort that would be taken by schemes of redistribution. If property were not already owned, no issue of *re*distribution would arise.

But seizing on the exact words while ignoring their sense, Cohen demurs. Property does *not*, he replies, initially come with claims of ownership attached. Rather, all property may be traced back to initial acquisition: before this, property was available for the taking.

No doubt; but what has happened to Cohen's challenge to the assumption that property begins as unowned? I suggest that the assumption has enough intuitive force to occlude Cohen's own challenge to this principle temporarily from his memory.[8] But whether or not I am right about the force of the strong version of the claim that property begins as unowned, the Lockean version need not assume its truth.

Suppose, however, that Cohen's argument against Lockean ownership were entirely right. What would ensue? In terms of an adequate response to the claim that capitalism, not socialism, promotes freedom: very little. Let us assume that, from birth, people acquire a certain share of their society's resources. These shares combine to block acquisition of unowned property: all property begins as owned. Though this starting point could hardly differ more from a Lockean account, what would spring from it is not socialism, but a form of capitalism. People would be free, once they were given their initial shares, to do with them as they wish. Cohen's argument against Nozick, while interesting, leaves untouched the issue we wish to consider here: the Marxist reply to the charge that capitalism promotes individual liberty. To respond by adducing a variant version of capitalism seems dubious.

Cohen himself knows full well that the assumption of initial ownership of all property by birth leads to a variant of capitalism. Hillel Steiner has advocated precisely this system, and Cohen defends Steiner against an objection posed by Ronald Dworkin.[9] It is a matter for some surprise, then, that Cohen fails to see the very limited value of the point he has stressed so much against the Lockean theory.

Of course, one could counter this argument by asserting that the property rights people have from birth consist of nothing at odds with full-scale socialism. But this position cannot be maintained unless one drops self-ownership. Socialism does not restrict only the use people can make of property; it also restricts their use of their labor. In a system of central planning, this restriction takes place directly, since workers are usually assigned to their jobs. Other types of socialism also restrict labor; in market socialism, for example, people are not free to form capitalist firms. More generally, unless one can acquire and own property, self-ownership amounts to very little. As the libertarian authors mentioned previously have stressed, people need various items in order to survive and flourish. If these items are under the political control of others, those in control can drastically limit freedom. And the entire point of Cohen's challenge to Nozick begins from Cohen's acknowledgement of the strength of the case for self-ownership. Thus, Cohen has so far failed to refute the case for liberty under capitalism.

Cohen then opens fire on Nozick's version of the Lockean proviso, because he believes it to be the keystone of Nozick's theory. As Cohen construes it, the theory has this form: since each person owns himself, people are free to do anything that does not interfere with anyone else's right to self-ownership, so long as what one does leaves no one worse off. One may therefore acquire unowned property freely, so long as doing so leaves no one worse off.

Given self-ownership, then, the proviso obviously ranks as the crucial part of the account. But Cohen's presentation misconceives Nozick's analysis entirely.

Oddly, Cohen falls victim here to an obverse error to that of the one I earlier accused him. Before, I suggested that he wrongly imputed the idiosyncracies of Nozick's view to modern libertarians generally. Here, he saddles Nozick with positions that several other writers of libertarian persuasion have adopted.

To be more specific, some of the writers I listed above *do* think that the right to acquire unowned property stems from self-ownership. Since you own yourself, if you "mix your labor" or the equivalent with unowned property, it becomes yours.

Nozick's theory lacks this stress on self-ownership—a term, in fact, that he does not use. In his book, he only offers a placeholder for an acceptable principle of initial acquisition. Nozick, of course, believes that individuals possess rights that may not be violated for the sake of collective benefit. In this sense, Nozick indeed acknowledges the principle of self-ownership. But, against Cohen, he makes no attempt to derive the acquisition of unowned property directly from self-ownership.

Does this matter? Other libertarians *do* derive the rights to acquire property from self-ownership. This derivation forms the basis of (for example) Murray Rothbard's discussion in *Ethics of Liberty*. Why, then, concentrate on whether Cohen has been true to Nozick, so long as he has managed to state the gist of one interpretation of the libertarian argument?

But this is precisely the difficulty. By tying his argument to Nozick, Cohen has fallen between two stools. If I am right, he has attributed a position to Nozick that other libertarians adopt, not Nozick himself. But Cohen's case will not pass muster as an account of these other libertarians, either. Cohen describes other details of Nozick's position correctly and his discussion of them only fits Nozick, not others with allied views.

The most important example of the failure of Cohen's argument to address the "typical" libertarian argument concerns the Lockean proviso. Many libertarian theories omit this proviso entirely. The criticisms that Cohen makes of the proviso (discussed below) leave theories without this feature unscathed.

Furthermore, Cohen's construal of the libertarian argument for property acquisition prevents him from considering what seems to me a strong form of the argument. As Cohen presents the libertarian argument, the right to self-ownership implies the liberty to do whatever does not interfere with the rights of others. This liberty includes the right to acquire unowned property. While this is indeed part of the libertarian case, it omits the point—stressed by those in the Randian or neo-Aristotelian tradition—that the right to acquire property on an individual basis is essential to human survival and flourishing. If one grants the strength of the principle of self-ownership, then this consideration, if correct, offers a strong defense of property rights that Cohen ought to consider.

There is one other obstacle that bars the way to applying Cohen's analysis of Nozick to those who derive the right to acquire property from self-ownership. Theorists who take this line usually support some variant of "labor-mixture" as needed to acquire property. I don't wish to suggest that all of these writers support Locke's exact words on the subject. But they think that acquisition depends on one's performing some labor on unowned property.

Since Nozick's theory lacks this feature, as Cohen correctly notes, Cohen fails to address it. Thus, his case misfires whether Cohen argues against the self-ownership theorists or against Nozick. He attributes a position to Nozick that he does not hold but cannot address that position properly, since he entangles it with other propositions found only in Nozick's work.

With these caveats in mind, Cohen's remarks about the proviso repay close attention. Nozick thinks that one can acquire unowned property only if doing so leaves no one worse off than he was in the state of nature. Nozick's state of nature, unlike that of Thomas Hobbes, does not leave people in a "war of all against all." Instead, people generally respect the rights of others, but individual property does not yet exist.

Cohen's challenge to Nozick here comes as no surprise. Why does Nozick select this as the baseline? Why not select a higher baseline? Why not institute as the baseline a system in which one cannot prevent others from using one's property when one has no need for it?[10] Here, individual property in the full sense would be allowed only if it led to better results overall than this baseline. Innumerable other baselines might be chosen: why choose Nozick's?

Cohen's contention that Nozick's choice of his baseline is arbitrary rests on his virtual reduction of Nozick's theory of property acquisition to the proviso. If, contrary to fact, Nozick's whole theory of property acquisition did rest entirely on the proviso, as Cohen thinks, then Cohen's question would strike at the heart of the theory. Why *should* we pick just this baseline?

Additionally, on Cohen's construal the theory would allow this absurdity: someone who said "I hereby acquire any and all property that no one else has yet acquired, so long as my doing so leaves no one worse off" would obtain what he claims, since Cohen takes observing the terms of the proviso to be sufficient, instead of merely necessary, to acquire unowned property following Nozick's theory.

In fact, Nozick's theory barely resembles Cohen's presentation of it. Although he does not specify his principle of initial acquisition, Nozick makes clear that an adequate theory must incorporate a rule of this kind.[11] With this feature included, our assessment of Cohen's argument must change.

Nozick (in this respect typically Lockean) attaches considerable weight to his rule of initial acquisition. This is precisely the point of the low baseline. Because the principle of acquisition gives whomever meets its terms a strong claim to the property he secures through its application, little else is needed. To demand that one meet the standards of a high baseline as well would introduce into the theory a block to acquisition that would be difficult to withstand. The initial principle, though strong, would still need a great deal more to supplement it. Only if we start from the assumption that acquiring property ought to be of enormous difficulty would a double-strength postulate make sense. And no one inclined to a Lockean view in the first place will make people run an obstacle course in order to obtain property.

We may press the point one further step. Why include the proviso at all? On one construal of Nozick's account, the proviso has been called into being only in order to meet the fact (as Nozick takes it to be) that no one has yet arrived at a satisfactory principle of initial acquisition. The combination of *some* fairly plausible initial principle with the proviso forms the "closest instantiated realization" of an adequate principle of acquisition.[12] Were a good rule available, it would render the proviso otiose. If this is right, then the proviso, far from being the sum and substance of Nozick's position, need not even form part of it. But this reading of the theory is controversial, and I do not insist on it.

Cohen might well respond to the main line of argument we have urged against him: "Suppose that a Lockean theory does stress the principle of initial acquisition. The rules that Lockeans have arrived at then fall victim to Nozick's strictures against the labor mixture principle. Each of the standard Lockean theories in this respect consists of no more than a slight shading of Locke's requirement of labor mixture."

The challenge has been fairly put. Has Nozick forever cast out Locke's time-honored theory from philosophical respectability? I do not think he intends such a drastic outcome. The famous case that some assume ruins Lockean labor mixture is the following: "If I own a can of tomato juice and spill it into the sea . . . do I thereby come to own the sea, or have I foolishly dissipated my tomatoe juice?"[13]

Let us more explicitly set out the difficulty this example raises for the principle of labor mixture. Suppose someone wishes to acquire some unowned property. On the Lockean theory, he owns his labor. If he does something with the property, he has joined what he owns (his labor) to something he does not yet own (the property). Why should one hold that the sum 'labor + unowned property' equals 'newly acquired property'? Why not hold instead that, at the end, one still owns one's labor while the property continues to be unowned? 'Labor' here, of course, refers to someone's activity, rather than to what he produces through his activity. What occupies us now is the question of whether he has acquired what he has made by his labor.

Nozick's penetrating example does not require one to abandon labor mixture either in intention or result. I suggest two responses that support the Lockean principle. I have briefly cited the first of these in another context. If people could not acquire property at all, the result would be universal destruction. *Any* theory of property, not just a Lockean one, must enable people to end up with property, unless one agrees with Eduard von Hartmann that the extinction of the human race is desirable.[14]

One might respond to this by saying that not every (nonsuicidal) theory of distribution need allow property in the full sense. The right to property, as Lockeans understand it, permits owners to exclude others unconditionally from the use of their (that is, the owners') possessions. Why not instead adopt a system lacking this feature—for example, one in which someone can use any object no one else is currently using? In this view, "owners" do *not* possess strong powers to bar others from their property.

The question just raised strikes home—if our present task were the construction of a theory of property. Fortunately, it is not. Nozick's example does not leave the use theory unscathed, either. Why does someone who mixes his labor with unowned property acquire the right to own it in the limited way this doctrine envisions? The suicide argument offers a reply to this view as well as the Lockean one. Even if it is not logically necessary to hold that one acquires previously unowned property if one mixes one's labor with it, the case for property acquisition is nevertheless strong. If "mixture" results in the "loss" of one's labor, human survival is imperiled, since (as mentioned before) one needs access to things in order to survive. Anyone who wishes to remain alive has a compelling reason to reject the "lose your labor" alternative.

A somewhat more technical issue also suggests a response to Nozick's example which supports property acquisition. Let us recall the terms of the problem: you own your labor, but property is unowned. The latter clause contains the key to the riddle. It does not say "property is unownable"; this reading obviously begs the question. Instead, the proper reading is that the property has not *yet* been acquired.

Of course, I do not mean here that, to solve Nozick's problem, we ought to take for granted that mixing one's labor with unowned property suffices to secure it. To do so also begs the question. Rather, we assume nothing at all about the property except that, prior to labor mixture, it is unowned. In particular, let us for the present make no prior assumption about whether unowned property can ever become owned.

At first, one might think this tactic renders Nozick's problem incapable of resolution. On the contrary, it opens the door to an answer. If we do not know whether unowned property can be owned but do know that each person owns his labor, an asymmetry has arisen. We have knowledge in one case and ignorance in the other.

If, then, one faces the choice that either one acquires unowned property by mixing one's labor with it or one loses one's labor, an answer on quasi-formal grounds lies at hand. Since we *do* know that each person owns his labor and do *not* know that property cannot be acquired, a Lockean resolution of the problem is indicated. To put the problem in a slightly different way, Nozick asks why ownership of labor and mixture of labor with unowned property equal ownership of property? Why does the positive quality (I own my labor) determine the result rather than the negative feature? (The property is unowned.) Why not: labor mixture + unowned property = unowned property altered by labor? The answer I have suggested is that one should take the "equation" in the Lockean way, because the quality of being unowned attributed to property does not work against a principle that allows its acquisition. All that has been said is that property is unacquired. To have a genuine paradox, one would need reason to think that property is unownable, not just unowned. Faced with *this* symmetry, quasi-formal considerations would avail us nothing, though the argument from the requirements of human survival still would settle the matter. Fortunately, though, this is not our situation.

Cohen cannot, then, remove the labor mixture theory from consideration by appeal to Nozick. And if one accepts some presently available version of labor mixture as "good enough" to justify property acquisition, Cohen's quandaries over the proper baseline cease to trouble us. On a pure labor-mixture position (not, incidentally, Locke's own position), no proviso exists at all. People can acquire property without having to determine the effect of their acquisition on others, so long as doing so violates no rights of others. To advocate or criticize this position cannot occupy us now: our sole task is to attend to Cohen's arguments against a capitalist system of property. I allow myself, however, one quick point. If one is inclined to dismiss a Lockean theory without the proviso as too harsh, recall that many generally-accepted exercises of rights make others worse off. Someone whom you dislike may move into your neighborhood; someone may publish opinions you find upsetting; even more directly on point, someone may drive you out of your job by virtue of his better qualifications. (This may take place under most socialist regimes: I do not here assume the existence of capitalism.)

We cannot, however, at once abandon Cohen and, even if so inclined, accept a Lockean approach. Cohen directs several further objections against the theory. The first of these rests on an appeal to ethical intuition. Cohen devises a situation in which it appears that Nozick's theory allows acquisition of unowned property. The case, however, exerts strong pressure on us to condemn the takeover of property as unacceptable, Nozick's account to the contrary notwithstanding.

The case is this. Two people live on an island. One of them cultivates a part of the island by himself but has not claimed this land as his property. His more enterprising fellow resident, already the owner of part of the island, now adds the first person's land to his own appropriation. He scrupulously obeys the proviso by hiring the other man for an amount slightly higher than the latter earned by his solitary activity.

Prima facie, Cohen thinks, the expropriator has validly acquired his new property by Nozick's theory. The expropriator has not made the other islander worse off. He thus meets the terms of the Lockean proviso. As Cohen views Nozick's account, this is sufficient to justify his acquisition. But must we not condemn the outcome as unfair nevertheless? Surely, Cohen maintains, the initial user of the land cannot be reduced to an employee of someone else on his land, just because he suffers no financial loss. Of course, he need not accept the offer of wages—but then the appropriator, now the owner of the land, may expel him from it altogether.

In fact, Cohen's example leaves Nozick's account, as well as the other main contending Lockean theories, untouched. The force of the example rests on the dubious assumption that the first cultivator has not acquired the land on which he works. But why make so odd a supposition? Nothing in any of the Lockean theories requires that one make an explicit claim to own property one endeavors to acquire. The point at issue emerges clearly if we first consider the labor-mixture view. The cultivator, by the terms of the example, has worked the land: why does he not then own it?

Since Nozick does not spell out a principle of just initial acquisition, Cohen's case is not quite so easy to settle. But the matter really presents little difficulty. Cohen has no basis on which to assume that Nozick would allow appropriation of the hapless cultivator who has neglected to claim his land explicitly. Surely someone who has worked by himself on some parcel of land over an extended period has acquired it; any reasonable principle of appropriation would adduce this as a paradigm case. And even if one shrinks from so definite a conclusion, Cohen still has no grounds for his assumption that Nozick's theory permits the counterintuitive result he constructs from his example, since Nozick does not discuss the case.

The trouble, once more, stems from Cohen's incorrect belief that the proviso forms the sum and substance of Nozick's theory. Since the appropriator meets the terms of the proviso, he "owns" the land he has taken on Cohen's construal of the theory. Cohen has altogether forgotten what the proviso has been designed as a proviso *to*—a principle of initial appropriation.

And even on Cohen's misreading, his conclusion does not follow. The initial cultivator also meets the terms of the proviso, since his use of the land does not worsen anyone's position. Why then does he not own the land?

Before turning from this topic, I pause to note a useful point about rights which Cohen's example brings to attention. To exercise a right generally requires no explicit claim that one possesses the right, or even an awareness that one has it. If someone practices a religion that others in his neighborhood do not like, he need not say "I hereby claim my right to freedom of religion" in order to be free from the interference of nonbelievers. He does not even have to know that his activities fall under a protected category.

This point, however, cannot be used directly to overthrow Cohen. It does not follow from what has just been said that *no* exercises of rights depend on explicit claims. But given the absence of a general argument, Cohen has the task of showing why an explicit claim must be made to acquire property.

Although in my opinion Cohen's case fails, I do not challenge his intuition that if Nozick's theory did have the consequences he deduces from it, the theory would produce an unfair result. The final point of those that Cohen raises against Nozick that I wish to consider, however, leads to a direct clash of beliefs.

Here Cohen directly addresses the issue of central concern to us: how, if at all, could a socialist reply to the claim that capitalism promotes liberty while socialism unduly restricts it? Cohen notes that, on Nozick's account, inequalities of wealth and income will almost certainly exist. Even if not present at the start, they will quickly ensue: Nozick's famous Wilt Chamberlain example shows that even very small transactions, if enough people engage in them, will have strongly inegalitarian results. (In the example, a large number of people pay Chamberlain 25¢ to play basketball. Although each person's expense is insignificant, Chamberlain winds up with a very large income.)[15]

Cohen directly confronts the point of the case: he denies that people need to be allowed to proceed unhindered to spend small sums of money as they wish. What if the majority of people in a society supports an egalitarian rule of distribution? Why may they not act to prevent people from acting in ways that will upset the system they prefer?[16]

To Cohen's question, we reply with a question of our own: why are those who support equality justified in imposing their preferences on others who do not share them? (If *everyone* wishes an equal distribution of property, nothing in a Lockean rule forbids a voluntary agreement to this effect.)

Cohen may believe that inequality will result in an undesirable state of affairs: for example, it may lead to a system in which workers are forced to labor for capitalists. This problem will be addressed in the next chapter. Alternatively, Cohen may oppose inequality because of the value he attaches to equality: whether or not inequality produces some *other* bad state of affairs, it is bad in itself. (Of course, both alternatives are compatible.)

I do not propose to discuss in detail here the question of whether equality is good or bad, and, if the former, to what extent its value justifies interference with freedom of economic action. Cohen's advocacy of equality allows us to see the full force of a point that arose earlier in our discussion. Any proposed rule of distribution requires support by argument. If Cohen favors an egalitarian rule, he assumes the task of coming up with reasons in its behalf. He cannot rightfully reject Lockean approaches simply on the grounds that they conflict with some other rule of distribution: *any* rule will contradict competing rules.

The point just raised sounds trivial: everyone knows that a controversial theory needs argumentative support. Far from being too minor to deserve discussion, the point strikes at a crucial weakness in Cohen's discussion. Cohen takes for granted that collective ownership of a society's resources forms the starting point of analysis.

In what way does he do this? As emerged from his treatment of the problem of the baseline, he assumes that individual appropriation of property ought to meet stringent terms. People possess in the state of nature the right to employ resources without appropriating them for their exclusive use. A Lockean rule must then show it has "better" results than this system: to accomplish this task, further, requires advocates of private property to take account of preferences of people for equality.

But why must Lockeans meet these demands, unless it has first been shown that an egalitarian, common-use system is the natural starting point from which all deviations have to be justified? Cohen in effect starts from the assumption of collective ownership of assets in a society. (Here "ownership" designates physical control, rather than a legally specified relation.)

This seems unfair. If one places a rule of distribution under scrutiny, one cannot legitimately assume that if the rule fails to justify itself, some other rule will automatically be in effect. All rules of distribution stand in the dock awaiting trial.

John Roemer, whose theory of exploitation we discussed in the previous chapter, also assumes that individualist ownership requires justification in a way that a collectivist system does not. Unlike Cohen, he devotes little effort to arguing against Nozick or other libertarians; on the present topic he thus calls for but brief treatment.

Roemer contends that, starting with unequal assets, a society of self-employed proprietors will be transformed into one in which some find it profitable to work for others.[17] He describes this situation as exploitative. He extends his analysis through his "General Theorem of Exploitation," in which a group counts as exploited if its situation would improve by secession from society, taking with it its proportionate share of the society's assets.

Once more, the question of the goodness or badness of equality does not here require a direct response. Rather, I mention Roemer to draw attention to his implicit assumption that unequal shares of assets with its attendant Roemerian exploitation alone require justification. Why assume without argument that an *equal* distribution of assets need not justify itself against an unequal initial position? Similarly, in the General Theorem, why does Roemer assume that a group has a valid claim to a share of total resources in proportion to its numbers? He may reply that he does not do this: he simply offers a definition of exploitation. But unless coalitions in fact *have* a claim to a share of total resources, what is the point of the whole analysis?

In this chapter, I have attempted to show that Cohen has not overthrown the *prima facie* case for laissez-faire capitalism on grounds of freedom. His attempt to do so depends on challenging the justice of capitalist property arrangements. If these are morally unacceptable, freedom of exchange under capitalism rests on a rotten foundation. Cohen's case proceeds by means of a detailed analysis of the theory of property held by Robert Nozick, the most famous academic libertarian. Cohen's arguments for the injustice of individual property acquisition fail. He misconstrues Nozick's theory and wrongly assumes it to represent all Lockean views. Cohen's analysis assumes without argument that a Lockean rule must pass a more severe argumentative standard than a collectivist rule. Roemer joins him in this dubious premise.

5

Cohen on Proletarian Unfreedom

In the preceding chapter, I attempted to show the failure of Cohen's and Roemer's arguments against the justice of individual ownership of productive property. This chapter is devoted primarily to another argument critical of capitalism. This argument, devised by G. A. Cohen, deals with the freedom of proletarians living in developed economies such as Britain and the United States.[1] Cohen maintains that proletarians in these economies are "collectively unfree" to leave the proletariat and that this lack of freedom is important. This chapter will also address another aspect of Cohen's multifaceted assault upon capitalism: his suspicion that the system prevents people from fully putting their preferences for leisure into effect.

Cohen's argument about collective unfreedom is important, because it strikes against a principal contention of this book. It has been argued here that, other things being equal, capitalism has this advantage over socialism: in it, people are free to arrive at whatever contracts about work they wish, so long as their agreements violate no one's rights. Under socialism, on the other hand, people work according to the directives of the economy's planners. If someone refuses to obey the plan, he can be compelled to do so on pain of legal punishment. If Cohen is right, workers under capitalism lack a crucial freedom; the defense of capitalism just given must then either be modified or abandoned. The argument about preference for leisure also weakens our case. If it is correct, in another vital respect people living in a capitalist economy do not have all the freedom the argument of this book imputes to them.

Are workers who live in a developed capitalist economy forced to labor for capitalists? In one sense, obviously not. The state does not use or threaten to use force against laborers who do not wish to work at all, or who do not wish to work for capitalists. Workers can start their own businesses with perfect legal freedom, or they can band together with others and form cooperatives. Further, the legal freedom of employment does not pass out of existence if a large number of workers prefer not to work for capitalists. Can Cohen's argument about collective unfreedom, then, be quickly dismissed?

In large part, it cannot. Cohen is fully aware that a worker who refuses to work for a capitalist employer faces no threat of force. He replies by adopting a more extended version of coercion, one based on an "economic structural constraint" which leaves workers no reasonable alternative but capitalist employment. The constraint in question, he suggests, exists in part because the state sustains the capitalist system:

> For the structure of capitalism is not in all senses self-sustaining. It is sustained by a great deal of deliberate human action, notably on the part of the state. And if, as I often think, the state functions on behalf of the capitalist class, then any structural constraint by virtue of which the worker must sell his labour-power has enough human will behind it to satisfy the stipulation that where there is force, there are forcing human beings.[2]

The meaning of this passage is not entirely clear. Cohen, as we are about to see, thinks that most workers in a capitalist system face no reasonable alternative to work for capitalists; this is the sense in which they are collectively unfree. The citation just given *may* mean that if people wished to shift to a system without this "structural constraint"—for example, an economy largely controlled by workers' cooperatives—the state would use force to prevent this. (We assume that workers in this system will usually work in firms they themselves own: otherwise, they will still be working for "others"—that is, for cooperatives in which they have no shares.)

If Cohen means this, his conclusion will be less significant than he thinks even if his main argument works. He attempts to show that workers are "collectively unfree" to leave the proletariat. But if he is right, why is it that workers do not alter this state of affairs? If the answer is that the state will use force against them if they try, then one wonders why Cohen has emphasized the details of his sense of unfreedom, a sense that allegedly involves no force.

There *is* force in his model—at one remove, rather than immediately. Surely, if workers are collectively placed in an unfavorable position that they are forbidden to alter, it is this latter fact that is decisive. Why go to a great deal of trouble (how much, we are about to see) to establish a sense of coercion *not* involving force if the whole system depends on the use of force in the ordinary sense?

However, it would be wrong to dismiss Cohen so quickly. The passage may mean only that the state will prevent people from using force to deprive capitalists of their ownership in the means of production. If this is all Cohen means, it is indeed necessary for defenders of capitalism to consider his argument in detail, since supporters of that system think that the ownership rights of capitalists *should* be protected.

Before turning to collective unfreedom, one more point regarding the use of force needs to be considered. Suppose that Cohen's argument works only if the state uses force in the first sense distinguished above—that is, if the state prevents people from changing the circumstance in which most workers work for capitalists. The following problem then arises for Cohen. The situation he has in mind is a counterfactual: "if workers attempted . . ., then the state would do . . ." How does he know that the state *would* prevent workers, say, from establishing cooperatives extensively if workers so far have not done so?

One reason for asserting this is that the state, in the words of the familiar Marxist slogan, is the "executive committee of the ruling class." If the interests of capitalists are threatened, the state will use force to defend them, crushing workers' desires to alter the existing order.

If this is Cohen's reason for thinking the state would prevent workers from changing to a system in which employment by capitalists was not dominant, then he has not succeeded in his task. He has not shown unconditionally that workers are collectively forced to work for capitalists. Rather, he has shown this to be true if one accepts an important component of Marxism. This hardly seems worth the trouble: it is not much in dispute that, *on the Marxist view*, workers find themselves subordinate to capitalists. The significant question is whether workers under capitalism

are unfree, even if one does not assume controversial doctrines of how the state operates.

Cohen is at least partially aware of this objection. He thinks that a less bold claim than the Marxists' view of the state suffices to support his argument. So long as the state maintains the "prevailing order,"[3] it will act to prevent workers from changing this. It need not act to preserve the prevailing order on the grounds that it is capitalistic.

Although Cohen's view that the state has an interest in preserving stability appears eminently plausible, his point does not refute the objection. Cohen assumes that in a capitalist economy, most workers must be employed by capitalists: a developed economy, he notes, requires a large proletariat.[4] If one does not assume this, the state need not act against workers attempting to change the prevalent mode of employment. Why assume that the stability of the "prevailing order" requires a large proletariat?

To revert to an earlier example, suppose that workers, disliking work under capitalists, set up large numbers of cooperatives. If they do so gradually, why will their activity disrupt the prevailing order? It will do so if there cannot be a capitalist system without an extensive proletariat, as Cohen claims. This, once again, is a Marxist doctrine which cannot properly be assumed as given. Cohen's reply to the objection—that his argument presupposes the Marxist doctrine of the state itself—presupposes another Marxist doctrine.

Cohen may mean, however, that as he defines capitalism, the system requires a large proletariat. If so, a system of cooperatives would not be capitalist by definition. But this would not show that the prevailing order requires that capitalism exist in this sense.

Unless, then, Cohen means to restrict his remarks about force to protection of the property rights of capitalists by the state, his entire argument rests on controversial assumptions about the state's use of force.

His argument for collective unfreedom is nevertheless significant and interesting. Against the obvious point, already mentioned, that individual workers are not legally compelled to labor for capitalists, Cohen replies that one can be unfree even if one is

not subject to force or its threat. If someone has no reasonable alternative to doing A, he is unfree not to do it. "Reasonable," although not exactly defined, takes account of normal human desires and exercises of rational thought. I am not free to refuse to eat for an extended period of time, assuming that I have the normal human desire to continue living and am aware that my eating is necessary to do this. Workers in this usage are unfree not to work since the alternatives, simply doing nothing or going on permanent relief, are either suicidal or degrading.

As Cohen recognizes, it does not follow from the fact that someone is forced to work that he is forced to work for a capitalist. In fact, in developed capitalist economies many workers manage to establish businesses of their own—ranging from repair shops, groceries, and restaurants to giant businesses like Apple Computer. It is *prima facie* the case, then, that workers are free under capitalism to refuse to work for a capitalist.

It would not be a good objection to this point that starting one's own business often requires protracted saving and restriction of consumption, and that operating one's own business is difficult and risky in any case. It is not a requirement of being free not to do A that one has low-cost or low-risk alternatives to A. So long as there are alternatives "within reach," one is not forced to do A.

Cohen, far from being defeated, has just begun to fight. He contends that in developed economies, only a few "exits from the proletariat" are available. Only a small proportion of the proletariat can set up businesses on its own. In a developed economy, mass production is the order of the day; most workers, then, must work for capitalists.

As Cohen again recognizes, this (even if true) still does not show that anyone is forced to work for a capitalist. However limited the number of exits may be, there is no unfreedom so long as everyone who wishes to leave the proletariat and work for himself can do so.

It is here that Cohen's most original point enters the scene. Even if everyone who wishes to leave is able to do so, the proletariat collectively cannot. Since only a few exits are available, the fact that an individual is free to leave depends on it being true that most workers do not wish to leave.

An example will clarify Cohen's point. Suppose that almost everyone is free to eat at the neighborhood restaurant; few find that prices impose an insurmountable obstacle to doing so. Still, the fact that everyone is free to eat there depends on the further fact that everyone does not wish to eat there at the same time. If the entire neighborhood descended on the restaurant, most people could *not* be served.

Similarly, if most proletarians wished to leave, they would in large part be doomed to disappointment. The condition of *my* leaving is that most of you do not; the condition of everyone's being free to leave is that most people do not wish to do so.

This completes the initial sketch of Cohen's argument. Before turning to an analysis of it, however, one topic requires attention. Suppose the argument is right. Why does the conclusion matter? Many cases of collective unfreedom are inconsequential. The example of the restaurant offers a clearcut case: the fact that we cannot all eat there at the same time is of trivial significance.[5]

Cohen, alive to this point, thinks that collective unfreedom to leave the proletariat is of great importance. Selling one's labor to a capitalist is a very undesirable state of affairs: in effect, one sells part of oneself.[6] The fact that a large class of people cannot collectively refrain from doing so is not a matter to be taken lightly. Further, the existence of collective unfreedom may affect the wishes of particular workers to exit from the proletariat. Some who might otherwise wish to do so will be constrained by feelings of class solidarity. They will be unwilling to leave unless their fellow workers accompany them.

Cohen's ingenious argument stands open to objection on a number of grounds. First, he deals in too cavalier a fashion with Robert Nozick's contention that having no reasonable alternative to doing A is not a sufficient condition for being unfree to do A. Nozick offers the case of someone who wishes to marry but finds that because all other eligible persons are already spoken for, only one person is available—and marriage to this person is barely preferable to remaining single. Nozick thinks it wrong to say that the person, so long as he wishes to marry, is coerced into marrying the one available choice. The restricted choice available comes about because of the legitimately exercised preferences of others.

He thinks that in order to show that someone is coerced to do A, one must show that his options have been unjustly restricted.[7]

Cohen gives Nozick's point short shrift. He claims it leads to the "absurd upshot"[8] that someone who is justly imprisoned is not unfree to leave his cell. Since the jailor has acted within his rights, he has not coerced his prisoner.

Cohen, entirely correctly, thinks that an imprisoned person is unfree. But he wrongly believes that Nozick disagrees. Nozick's restriction on coercive acts to those in which someone violates another's rights applies only when force or its threat is unused. If either or both are, Nozick does not impose the restriction to which Cohen objects.

Nozick's reasoning appears to be something like this. If one restricts coercion to cases involving force or threat of same, one can dismiss claims at once that workers are compelled to labor for capitalists. No one makes them do it. Marxists and others who believe that workers are forced to work for capitalists think that this definition dismisses their claim too quickly. In partial concession, Nozick allows some cases to count as coercive which do not involve the use or threat of force. In these cases, someone restricts another's alternatives when he has no moral right to do so. An example of what Nozick has in mind might be blackmailing someone to prevent him from doing business with someone else. The person who is unable to do business has had his alternatives restricted through morally impermissible means.

He thinks that allowing any case in which someone faces only one reasonable alternative to count as an instance of coercion goes too far. Thus his "moralized" approach is a compromise between Cohen's sort of definition of coercion and a "strict" definition. His marriage example seems to me to tell strongly against the definition Cohen uses. In the example, someone has no reasonable alternative in a very important area of life. Yet it seems wrong to say that he has been forced into his undesirable situation. Thus, even if Cohen's argument succeeds in showing that workers are collectively unfree to depart from the proletariat, he would still require an additional argument to show that they have been coerced. Since, as I shall try to show, Cohen's argument fails on its own terms, further resort to this point will not be necessary.

To turn to Cohen's own argument, his conclusion does not follow from his premises. Very briefly, here is his case. (1) In a developed capitalist economy, only a few exits from the proletariat are available. (2) The number of workers exceeds by far the number of exits. (This follows from (1) and the uncontroversial fact that developed capitalist economies contain a large proletariat.) (3) Not all proletarians can exit from the proletariat (by (1) and (2)). (4) The proletariat is collectively unfree to leave (by (3) and the definition of collective unfreedom).

The most obvious formal defect of the argument occurs in the derivation of (4). Cohen attempts to show that not all workers *can* exit from the proletariat. This is to say that if all or most workers attempted to leave, most of them would fail. Why would they fail? Because there would not be enough non-proletarian jobs for all those who wanted them. The proposition "If all or most workers attempted to leave the proletariat, they would largely fail" is, then, a counterfactual. It advances a claim about what *would be* the case if something *were* to occur.

Cohen's premise (1), however, is a claim about the actual world: in a developed capitalist economy, there *are not* many exits available from the proletariat. It does not follow from this that the claim about the contrary-to-fact situation is true. How does Cohen know that if all or most workers wished to exit from the proletariat, they would mostly fail? Premise (3) does follow from (1) and (2): if there are more workers than exits, some workers will not succeed in leaving. Crucially, however, (4) does not follow from (1), (2), and (3). The premise "The proletariat is unfree to leave" is true only if the counterfactual "If most workers wanted to leave, they would fail" is true. For *this* to be true, it must be the case that there *would not* be enough exits. It is insufficient to claim that there *are not* enough.

An example Cohen uses in explaining collective unfreedom may make this criticism clearer. Against those who question the significance of collective unfreedom, Cohen gives this case. A hotel,

> at which one hundred tourists are staying, lays on a coach trip for the first forty who apply, since that is the number of seats in the

coach. And suppose that only thirty want to go. Then, on my account, each of the hundred is free to go, but their situation displays a collective unfreedom. Yet it seems wrong, the objector says, to speak of collective unfreedom here. I do not agree. For suppose all of the tourists did want to go. Then it would seem appropriate to say that they are not all free to go. . . . The coach case is a rather special one. For we tend to suppose that the management lays on only one coach because they correctly anticipate that one will be enough to meet the demand. Accordingly, we also suppose that if more had wanted to go, there would have been an appropriately larger number of seats available.[9]

Cohen here presents clearly and exactly the point that has been raised against him. Yet he never applies the point to his own argument about proletarian unfreedom. He never asks: how many exits from the proletariat would be available, if all or most workers wanted to leave?

Perhaps Cohen would reply that it is obviously true that the number of exits would be insufficient to allow most workers to leave. But if workers wish not to be employed by capitalists, then small businesses offering partnership positions or cooperatives would have a competitive advantage over capitalist firms. Because workers wish to avoid the latter sort of employment, they will be willing to accept lower remuneration in the former sort of establishment. Of course, if workers are willing to leave the proletariat only if their income does not decrease, this is another matter. But the important case seems to be: are workers free to exit the proletariat if they are willing to pay the price for doing so?

Cohen might reply here that even if workers will accept lower income, there still will not be enough exits. A developed capitalist economy requires large-scale production; if there were "too many" small businesses, the standard of living would drastically decline.

This reply does not meet the point. It is not obvious that workers' cooperatives have to be small. Further, as Chapter 6 will illustrate, Cohen and others argue that a capitalist economy makes it difficult for cooperatives to get started. In this argument, "cooperative" is taken in its strict sense to mean a business which is owned equally by all those who work in it. Many other arrangements that are not cooperatives in this sense, however, are not examples of proletarians working for capitalists. For example, workers might own a business without having equal shares. In trying to assess how many exits from the proletariat would be available if most workers wanted to leave, it therefore is vital that one consider more than just a very restricted number of options.

Cohen does not discuss in detail his assumption that only a few exits would be available. A reasonable conjecture is that he assumes that the state would prevent a mass exodus from the proletariat. If this contention lies behind his argument, the problem discussed at the beginning of this chapter arises. On this interpretation, Cohen's argument works only if one adds in a controversial assumption about the state.

The argument for collective unfreedom suffers from another formal defect. Premise (2) seems most plausibly taken as a statement about how many exits and workers exist at a given time: there are now, for instance, X number of openings. If (2) is taken this way, at most (3)' rather than (3) follows, where (3)' is "Not all proletarians can *at the present time* exit from the proletariat." (Because of the counterfactual difficulty just raised, (3)' does not actually follow, but this is here placed to one side.) (3)' is compatible with all current proletarians exiting *at some time or other*. Those in the proletariat who could not currently leave because of the limited number of jobs available might simply have to wait their turn, and similarly for new workers who join the proletariat. The fact that non-proletarian positions do not await all of them *now* proves nothing about whether they are free to leave at some point in their career. This objection holds true even if one does not challenge Cohen's view that the number of exits from the proletariat is fixed. In fact, it is much more plausible to think that exits are expandable at the inclination of workers to leave. This was the point of the "counterfactual" objection.

Cohen partially recognizes this criticism, but he backs away from its implications. He states:

> Now when Marxists say that proletarians are forced to sell their labour-power, they do not mean: 'X is a proletarian at time t only if x is at t forced to sell his labour-power at t' for that would be compatible with his not being forced to at time t + n, no

matter how small n is. . . . The manifest intent of the Marxist claim is that the proletarian is forced at t to *continue* to sell his labour-power, throughout a period from t to t + n, for some considerable n.[10]

Cohen neglects to note the implications of his own statement. If what is important in determining freedom to leave the proletariat is the time interval $t + n$, it is wrong to consider the number of exits available at some given time t. This is exactly what Cohen does, however, since he deals with the number of exits that are currently available. One further clarification of this argument is needed. The point against Cohen is *not* that there are *now* only a comparatively few exits from the proletariat, but that at some future time this will cease to be true. Rather, even if it is true for every time t that there are then only a few exits available, it does not follow that any worker is forced to remain in the proletariat. The various exits that are available at each time need not be occupied by the same people. The fact that new positions are continually coming up may give everyone in the proletariat a chance to leave, even if at any given time not everyone can do so.

None of this shows, however, that it will in fact work out that everyone in the proletariat is free to leave. But if one takes into account that the average worker will be employed for over forty years (that is, ages 20–65), one cannot simply take for granted, as Cohen does, that exits will be insufficient to enable all proletarians to leave. It would not be a good reply to this that if someone has to wait forty years to leave the proletariat, his freedom to leave does not amount to much. A proletarian who wishes to leave does *not* have to wait a long time to do so. Cohen does not challenge this, at least for the purpose of his collective unfreedom argument. Cohen's claim is that although individual workers are free to leave, this depends on most workers' inability to do so. The argument just given, if successful, weakens Cohen's claim. At most, his argument shows that not all workers are free to exit in a short amount of time.

Cohen's argument thus fails. To derive (4), "The proletariat is collectively unfree to leave," he requires a counterfactual premise unlike (2), like "The number of workers exceeds by far the number of exits that would be available if all or most workers wanted to leave." Further, on the most plausible construal of (2), the argument fails for an additional reason: it considers only exits available at given times, rather than the number of exits that will arise in the course of a worker's career. To deal with this point, Cohen needs a premise like this: "The number of workers at t exceeds the number of exits that will become available during the length of the working lives of those who are workers at t." (Of course, if Cohen means just this by (2) rather than the construal given it here, what reason do we have to think (2) true on this reading?) Combining the two requirements, Cohen needs the following for his argument to work: (2) "The number of workers at time t exceeds the number of exits that would become available during the working careers of workers at time t, if all or most of these workers wished to leave the proletariat." And for *this* premise, Cohen has given no argument at all.

It will be recalled that in addition to arguing for the collective unfreedom of the proletariat, Cohen also maintains that this lack of freedom is important. Because workers employed by capitalists have to subordinate themselves to their employers, the condition of being in the proletariat is very undesirable. Thus, although many cases of collective unfreedom (for example, our restaurant example) are inconsequential, this one is not. Having criticized the validity of Cohen's argument, I now want to question the importance of its conclusion.

Cohen thinks that workers have to subordinate themselves: others gain control of their "productive existence." First, it is not clear how the situation of a worker differs in this respect from that of people in a simple barter economy where no Marxist exploitation is present. (We can, if we wish, assume equal resources at the start, so that Roemerian exploitation, discussed in Chapter 3, is not present either.) Suppose that A and B own land on which both wheat and barley can be grown. A finds it most to his advantage to grow wheat on his land and exchange it for barley grown by B. If one asks why A grows wheat, the answer is in part that B wants wheat. Similarly, B grows barley because A wants it. From the fact that A and B each produce something that someone else wants, it does not follow that either is subordinate to the other.

The same conclusion appears true for the capitalist situation that concerns Cohen. Laborers are performing certain activities because their employers want them. In return, the employers advance wages to the workers. Where is the subordination here?

One place it is not to be found is in the fact that the workers are selling their labor, rather than exchanging products as in the example of the farmers. The wheat and barley in that example were not free goods; they required labor to cultivate. Why does it make a difference that, in one case, the product of labor is sold, and in the other, the activity of labor is sold? In each case, people are attempting to better their positions by exchange.

The case changes if one assumes that workers under capitalism are exploited. If Cohen means to include this as an implicit premise of his argument, it will once again rely on the truth of a controversial doctrine. In this instance, however, it is doubtful that Cohen wishes to take the Marxist view of labor exploitation for granted. As discussed in an earlier chapter, this view rests on the labor theory of value—and Cohen rejects the labor theory. Cohen may have in mind some other doctrine of exploitation. But if he does not, the question again arises: why does Cohen regard it as undesirable to work for a capitalist? Perhaps by "subordination," he means that the employer tells his workers how they are to labor. Workers do not decide what to produce and under what conditions they will work: the owner of the firm, whether directly or through subordinates, gives the instructions. By contrast, in the former example neither A nor B instructs the other how to produce his crop.

This reply fails on two grounds. It is often true that employers state certain wages and conditions in a job offer, giving applicants the choice of accepting them or seeking employment elsewhere. This is by no means always the case, particularly in industries where labor unions are strong and extensive bargaining takes place before contracts are signed. But even if employers offer prospective employees terms which they are free either to accept or reject, no subordination is necessarily present. The case is similar to that of buyers at a market with prices fixed by the seller. In most supermarkets, for example, a customer must either pay the price at which goods are offered for sale or shop elsewhere: no bargaining takes place in the store.

It is hardly true, though, that customers have no influence on food prices and are subordinate to the owners of the chains who set the prices. The goods offered for sale are priced according to estimates of what consumers will want: the fact that customers of a particular store do not bargain over price *in the store* hardly shows that demand has no influence on price.

Exactly the same is true for laborers. Employers will presumably offer conditions and wages that will attract employees. Whether wages and conditions are established through an explicit bargaining process does not appear to possess major significance. This is not to say that it is always irrelevant whether someone is a "price taker": only the weaker claim has been advanced that this is insufficient to show subordination. Since Cohen does not rest his argument on a non-competitive labor market, in which, at most, a very few firms offer employment (monopsony or oligopsony), a competitive labor market has been implicitly assumed.

Where, then, is the subordination? Perhaps Cohen thinks it arises from the fact that workers are compelled to labor for firms that aim at maximizing profit. Workers give up autonomy over an important part of their lives, since the constant pursuit of profit, the motor of capitalism, leaves no room for any goals in production in which workers may be interested other than economic efficiency. This argument, which Cohen does indeed adopt, will be discussed in more detail below. For now, it is important to remember that it does not follow from the capitalists' pursuit of profit that workers who want working conditions of a certain kind will be unable to secure them. If the conditions detract rather than add to productivity, of course there will be, *ceteris paribus*, an incentive not to adopt them. But if workers are willing to pay for these conditions by accepting lower wages, they can still get what they want. If, for example, workers do not want to work on an assembly line, they can secure work they find more varied and interesting—if they are willing to pay the price. The fact, if it is one, that the working conditions Cohen thinks reasonable are not those that maximize production is hardly the fault of capitalism: this is just the way the world is.

The last statement appears vague, but what is meant is easily clarified. After quoting Marx about the "dull compulsion" of labor under capitalism, Cohen speaks of "liberation from class society."[11] He appears to have in mind a state of affairs that is radically better than the prevailing capitalist order of things. One might envisage a system more efficient that capitalism or at least as efficient, in which work was always light and pleasant rather than sometimes dull and onerous. Alternatively, Cohen might be thinking of a system in which labor occupied only a small amount of time, in which people would have most of their days available for leisure.

One may readily admit that most people would find either of these systems an improvement over the present order. But what reason is there to think that change of this sort is possible? As mentioned in Chapter 1, Ludwig von Mises and Friedrich Hayek have claimed to demonstrate that a socialist economy cannot work. (One assumes the abandonment of class society of which Cohen speaks involves the onset of socialism.) These arguments seem to me to be persuasive; even if one rejects them, however, what reason is there to think that a socialist economy will be radically better than the capitalist sort? One suspects that behind Cohen's complaints of workers' subordination is an implicit denial that, given present technology and resources, much dull and unpleasant labor is necessary in a developed economy. Presumably, few people would like to work as garbagemen—but this fact will not make the garbage go away. Nor is garbage confined to capitalist economies.

Cohen may respond that in speaking of liberation from class society, he does not assume without evidence the existence of a utopian order. Instead, he might claim that so far his plain meaning has been ignored. Capitalists do not have to sell their labor power, while workers do (except, of course, for those who can escape the proletariat). A laborer is working *for* someone else—in most cases, someone who is not a laborer. Even if the employer works in his own business and earns "wages of management," he is still not working for someone else. Cohen's contention here seems entirely right—a worker employed by a capitalist *is* working for someone else. But this is the starting point of the whole question: exactly the problem that Cohen needs to solve is why the collective unfreedom of the proletariat matters, when other cases of collective unfreedom do not. It is hardly an adequate response merely to reiterate the situation that gave rise to the question in the first place.

Cohen might again respond that his point has been ignored. Just what he contends *is* the bad state of affairs is that most people have no reasonable alternative except labor while some—the capitalists, or a subset of that class—do not have to labor. (Perhaps some capitalists *do* have to work, but Cohen thinks that at least some very wealthy ones do not.) At this point the issue becomes difficult to discuss, as it appears to rest upon a value judgment. The question could be dealt with properly only within the context of an ethical system: the defense of one far exceeds the goal of this book. Perhaps one might note, though, that it is not obvious why the question of whether one is in a good or bad situation depends on whether others are much better off. Why is the fact that, under capitalism, some people do not have to work sufficient to show that those who do work are badly off?

One blind alley here is to bring forward the Marxist doctrine that capitalists have gained control of the means of production through violent expropriation. Suppose that, in the former example, A will buy B's barley with wheat he has not grown himself but has stolen from C. The fact that A is a thief does not tell us whether B's contract with A is good or bad. If capitalists ought not to own the means of production, this is one issue: it is dispositive of whether workers are in a desirable position.

There is another construal available of what Cohen objects to in the workers' subordination. Since one's employment is (for almost everyone) a very significant part of life, the existence of collective unfreedom becomes important by that fact alone. The point here may be grasped by returning to Nozick's example of the person who has only one available marriage partner. Even if one agrees with Nozick that no coercion is present, the person's condition certainly seems an undesirable one. In like manner, workers in capitalism are in a bad situation just because most of them have no reasonable choice except to labor. It is certainly undesirable not to have any choice over a major part of life.

If Cohen's collective unfreedom argument is right, then he is correct that most workers have to labor for capitalists. But it does not follow from the absence of this particular choice that workers do not have a wide variety of other important choices as regards their labor. Specifically, most laborers have a choice of whom to work for—if they dislike the conditions a particular firm offers, they are free to move elsewhere.[12]

It is virtually always possible to come up with cases of collective unfreedom, a point Cohen himself recognizes. Further—and *this* point Cohen seems to deny—it does not follow that because an instance of collective unfreedom affects an important area of one's life, it itself is important. It is probably true, for example, that most people in a developed economy are collectively unfree to leave the market altogether and become self-sufficient farmers. The demand of a large population for food cannot be met by small farmers alone. But why is the absence of this option important? It is not contended here that this example shows that Cohen's collective unfreedom is unimportant, or even that it is obviously the case that the collective unfreedom to become self-sufficient farmers is unimportant. All that is required is that one accept the weaker claim that the latter collective unfreedom may not be important. To the extent one thinks it is not, there is reason to reject the position that an instance of collective unfreedom in an important area of life is always itself important. And this leaves Cohen with a problem.

So far, then, we have concluded that Cohen has failed to show that workers are collectively unfree to leave the proletariat. Further, he has not proved his related claim that this collective unfreedom, if it exists, is important. We are now in a position to address another contention Cohen advances.

Although Cohen concedes that individual proletarians are free to leave for the purposes of the collective unfreedom argument, he at times hedges on his concession. He appears to avoid the question of whether workers are individually free to exit the proletariat. One can see why his argument presses him in this direction. If, as he contends, collective unfreedom to leave the proletariat is important primarily because working for a capitalist is "bad," why is it the case that most proletarians are not clamoring to get out? How can it be true that anyone who wants to leave the proletariat can do so? If proletarians were individually unfree to leave, Cohen could avoid this difficulty.

Although Cohen does not fully commit himself on the issue, he advances two points in his discussion that our earlier analysis permits us to challenge. He thinks that individual workers may find it an unreasonable alternative to leave the proletariat because to do so would strike a blow at "proletarian solidarity." Additionally, workers desiring liberation from class society may not find much appeal in the option of joining the "petty-bourgeoisie" by becoming small shopkeepers.

Neither of these points offers a good reason to see individuals as unfree to leave the proletariat. The desire to preserve "proletarian solidarity" and distaste for the petty-bourgeoisie are presumably predicated on the assumption that the capitalist class system is undesirable. If so, a question arises: what is wrong with it? The answer cannot *just* be that it forces workers to remain in the proletariat, if it is the case that they wish to preserve proletarian solidarity. This desire is rational only if there is something else wrong with the system. What is it? Cohen does not say.

Further, as Cohen himself recognizes, distaste for the petty-bourgeoisie is not sufficient to show that workers who feel this way are unfree to leave the proletariat. He replies to Chaim Tannenbaum, who contends that becoming a small businessman should not be considered a "real option," by modifying his conditions of unfreedom.[13] He now requires that to be unfree not to do A, any alternative to A must be substantially worse than A. If a worker, then, faces no reasonable alternative to remaining in the proletariat because he dislikes becoming a small businessman, this does not suffice to show his unfreedom. The alternative must be much more undesirable than his present condition. It is not enough that it be no better or even slightly worse.[14]

As before, Cohen has not recognized the full implications of his own case. If workers do not see the "petty-bourgeois" alternative as substantially worse, why is it not the case that more of them are trying to leave? If an alternative to A is seen as about as good as A, one would expect choosers to be indifferent between A and the alternative. If so, it is unlikely that if choosers *must* choose either

A or the alternative, a high proportion will wind up choosing one option rather than the other. This outcome would suggest little indifference.

Applying this point to Cohen's problem, if workers regard being a small shopkeeper as about as good an option as being a worker, one would expect that a fair number of workers would wish to exercise this option if they could. If they cannot, it is not the case that anyone who wants to can leave the proletariat, and this would have to be the case if collective unfreedom to leave the proletariat exists together with individual freedom to leave. If, however, most workers consider becoming a small shopkeeper much worse than remaining a worker, then most workers are unfree to exit from the proletariat. In this case, too, collective unfreedom apart from individual unfreedom does not exist. It appears, then, that Cohen has offered no good reason either to think that individuals are unfree to leave the proletariat because of feelings of distaste for the petty bourgeoisie or that collective unfreedom to leave can exist without individual unfreedom.

If the argument of this chapter is correct, ought one to "discard" altogether the notions of individual and collective unfreedom to exit the proletariat? Not entirely. The ideas seem to apply with perfect accuracy to a centralized socialist system.

In a socialist economy, the system operates through an economic plan devised by a Central Planning Board. Workers are assigned their jobs, and the wages and working conditions in them, according to the dictates of the planners. They are not free to bargain, as they are in a capitalist economy. Further, workers are not free (either individually or collectively) to leave their jobs and establish businesses or cooperatives run by themselves. They are unfree not just because these actions are economically unviable; the central plan's directives are legally enforceable. Here, not in capitalism, proletarians are forced to work. The point is not altered if the socialist system is democratic, or if the plan is controlled by workers rather than a bureaucratic ruling class as in the contemporary U.S.S.R. Each individual worker has no choice but to accept the job conditions he is offered. Whether he has a voice—with a large population, a necessarily small one—in approving the plan is irrelevant.

It is true, of course, that some socialist economies allow private enterprise to a limited extent. A socialist system may also rely in part on market pricing. To the extent the system is modified, the points made above may not apply. The extent of workers' freedom under various kinds of socialism require individual examination. This question will arise again in the following chapter, where cooperatives are discussed.

In addition to his collective unfreedom argument, Cohen raises a different (though related) problem for capitalism. This argument has been touched on earlier; it requires only brief consideration. Cohen contends that the capitalist economy does not adequately provide for leisure: it over-emphasizes production and wealth.[15] In saying this, Cohen is not judging the market by his own values; if he were, one might say to him, "You prefer that people increase their demand for leisure, but they do not share your preference." His point is more difficult to meet: he thinks the market does not accurately reflect people's own preference for leisure.

Capitalists engage in a constant struggle for profit. If a company offered more relaxed working conditions or greater opportunities for leisure, it would fall victim to more productive rivals. It would do so even if people were to desire more leisure. Thus, preference for leisure cannot be fully realized: the drive for more and more production will undercut it. So that people will not find this state of affairs unsatisfactory enough to demand change, people are inundated with consumer goods. Massive campaigns urge them to buy more than they "really" wish.

This argument fails at two points. It is undoubtedly true that capitalists aim at profit. But it does not follow from this that they do not have preferences for activities other than engaging in business. While a capitalist usually does need to hold his own with the competition, this does not imply that he must make as much profit as it is humanly possible for him to do; he does not have to devote all his working time to his business.

More importantly, the central defect of the argument has already been mentioned. A firm that offered employees more leisure need not therefore lose out in competition. Working conditions form part of wages: if workers prefer certain conditions and are willing to pay for them, they can do so by accepting lower salaries to obtain them. The firm that allowed more leisure would also have a lower wages-bill. How it would fare in competition cannot be determined *a priori*. The substantial and continual lowering of the work week since the Industrial Revolution hardly supports Cohen's belief that capitalism fails to provide people with the leisure they wish.

In conclusion, Cohen has failed to show that there is anything wrong with being a worker in a capitalist system. This makes the issue of how able workers are to leave the proletariat less important than Cohen imagines. In any event, he has not shown that workers are either individually or collectively unfree to leave. He also has not succeeded in demonstrating that capitalism cannot adequately supply leisure.

6

The Socialist Alternative

As we have seen, the analytical Marxists cling to one tenet of classical Marxism, however much else of Marxism they jettison. They contend that under capitalism, workers are exploited. (The meaning they attach to "exploitation" differs substantially from Marx's.) In previous chapters, I have endeavored to show that the analytical Marxists have failed to establish the proposition that exploitation indelibly taints labor relations on the free market.

Suppose, however, that Cohen, Elster, and Roemer are right. Further, let us assume that they are also correct that exploitation is an evil. Does it follow that capitalism ought to be replaced by some other economic system? Not necessarily. Unless one adopts the view that capitalist exploitation is so terrible that any conditions are preferable to it, capitalism still needs to be compared with its alternatives. The question of the best system must then become the focus of inquiry. In Lenin's famous words, "What is to be done?"

If, for example, capitalism turned out to be the only economic system capable of producing the goods and services needed for a modern society, the fact (if it is one) that exploitation of labor could not be avoided would therefore be outweighed; better exploitation than chaos.

The analytical Marxists, one suspects, would readily assent. They do not take an absolutist view, in which once one has shown a bad feature of capitalism, that system then passes from rational consideration. Quite the contrary: part of their argument against capitalism consists of the advocacy of alternative ways of operating the economy. The alternatives are socialist. Unfortunately, the analytic Marxists have not discussed socialism with as much detail as they have capitalism. The alternative to capitalism that has aroused the most discussion in the group is market socialism. The following discussion thus will focus on market socialism, although not all analytic Marxists have supported it. In it, workers' cooperatives—

119

instead of capitalists—own most firms. Various schemes of market socialism entail different roles for the state in planning the economy and coordinating the activities of its firms.

Jon Elster has been the most active advocate of market socialism in this group. Cohen has not fully committed himself, but he is sympathetic to it. Roemer, while not repudiating market socialism, refuses to abandon the centralized economic system that has traditionally been associated with Marxism. [1]

In this chapter, a brief account of the case against centralized socialism will be given. The arguments that Elster gives in favor of workers' cooperatives will then be examined. These are principally related to the importance of creative work and the alleged superiority of cooperatives over capitalist firms in securing it. Finally, I shall contend that most workers will find it in their interest to reject participation in cooperatives if they can instead work for capitalist firms.

Does it follow from this that capitalism is preferable to market socialism? Not quite. If the arguments that led us earlier to reject the Marxist analysis of exploitation are correct, then our case seems made. But, for now, we shall grant to the Marxist that capitalist exploitation counts strongly against the free-market economy. If so, does not the question become one of the balance of advantages between the problems of market socialism and those, like exploitation, that are present under capitalism? How can one decide between these systems in a non-arbitrary way?

At the end of this chapter, I will argue that the issue of what is best for the workers can be left to the workers themselves. In a capitalist economy, workers who wish to form cooperatives are free to do so. They are not only free legally—that is, no one can use force to prevent them from acting in this way—but they also possess the means and ability to achieve this goal. The argument to the contrary that workers under capitalism face near-insurmountable obstacles, should they wish to establish cooperatives, will be examined. I shall finally contend that if workers in a cooperative system can legally enter into capitalist employment relations, the system should not be regarded as an alternative to capitalism.

Our conclusion, then, is that free-market capitalism is superior to market socialism. Unless one adopts the paternalistic contention that workers cannot accurately judge what they prefer, the balance of advantages favors capitalism over its rival.

Our argument has an unexpected bonus. The best argument that capitalist exploitation exists of those earlier examined has been advanced by G. A. Cohen. He contends that workers in a free-market economy are collectively forced to labor for capitalists. If workers are free to form cooperatives, one main prop of Cohen's case collapses. Thus, if the argument of this chapter is sound, we can reiterate our previous conclusion with renewed strength—that the analytical Marxist claim that capitalists exploit workers ought to be rejected.

Karl Marx would probably have found the concern with market socialism a waste of time at best. Why not overthrow capitalism completely—and, in its place, install a regime of central planning? Since the appearance of a famous article by Ludwig von Mises in 1920 on collectivist planning, the debate over socialism has shifted dramatically from where Marx left it.[2]

Marx thought that socialism would permit the forces of production to grow to unheard-of heights. Mises argued that a socialist economy would not function at all. Mises went beyond some of his supporters, such as F. A. Hayek, who contended that a socialist economy would encounter severe problems. Mises regarded economic calculation as impossible under socialism. In order to manufacture production goods in a way that does not lead to total disaster, economic actors must decide which production goods should be manufactured and the most efficient way to do so.

The latter concern is not purely a matter of engineering. Usually, several different ways of producing a good are technologically possible; in W. H. Hutt's phrase, one needs to know what is the "least cost" method of production. If, for example, one wishes to construct a kitchen sink, should one use bricks made of platinum? Fairly obviously not: the answer comes not from engineering, though, but from our knowledge that this would involve a wasteful use of resources.

In most instances, how to produce efficiently is by no means obvious; in Mises's view, only a market economy can answer the question in an adequate fashion. Central planners would face myriad decisions on production and have no means to answer them. In a capitalist economy, production decisions are made with the guidance of the price system. Changes in price reflect changes in demand and supply. They indicate profitable opportunities for investment to the capitalist. The key to Mises's argument is that the price mechanism does not exist under socialism. Instead, the planners must settle production decisions by edict. Centralized socialism must inevitably result in "planned chaos."

Mises's article, developed and expanded in his *Socialism* (1922), at once set off a fast and furious controversy that even now shows no signs of abating. Although I find Mises's contention persuasive, it would be inappropriate simply to assume its truth here, and a full analysis of the various points at issue in the controversy would far exceed the scope of this chapter.

Among the many replies to Mises, the most popular (although not the only) response among economists to his economic calculation argument is that it is possible to have a market without capitalism. A "socialist" system in which non-capitalist firms bid for resources *can* solve the major problems of production efficiently. So, at any rate, contended Oskar Lange and Fred M. Taylor in influential articles published in the 1930s.[3] Their reply to Mises quickly became the dominant orthodoxy of mainstream economics; it probably remains so at present, although Mises's original argument has recently been making a strong comeback. Unreconstructed advocates of central planning—for example, Maurice Dobb—who deny that calculation poses a problem at all to a regime of central planning have become lonely voices crying in the wilderness. (Dobb, a teacher of generations of economists at Cambridge University, maintained this view from the 1930s to his death in the mid-1970s.) Even the once-popular solution to Mises's problem—solving the manifold equations required to determine a state of economic equilibrium by means of computers—has fallen on evil days, owing to the criticisms of Friedrich Hayek and others.

At present, then, the available alternatives for the operation of a complex modern economy appear to be reduced to two—capitalism and market socialism. This our capsule summary of the debate over the calculation argument has by no means proved; it has only been included to show why centralized planning will not be discussed. As mentioned earlier, most analytical Marxists concur in viewing market socialism as the alternative to capitalism, although they have paid little explicit attention to the calculation argument.

To turn, then, to the principal topic of our chapter, what is a cooperative? It is a firm owned entirely by its workers; it does not employ laborers who hold no share in it. The last proviso is necessary to block a worker-owned firm that employs workers as a capitalist enterprise does from counting as a cooperative. Strictly speaking, in a cooperative all workers own equal shares; for our purposes, however, firms with unequal shareholders will qualify as cooperatives so long as all workers in a firm have a substantial "stake" in it. The wider usage is adopted to give the advocates of market socialism the benefit of the doubt. Difficulties that arise just because of an equal ownership provision will not be charged to them.

One more matter of definition requires attention. A market socialist system will be taken here as one in which (at least) the great majority of production takes place in cooperatives. A system in which consumer goods, but not capital goods, are manufactured by cooperatives does not qualify. Although some control of the firms by a central authority is allowable in a market socialist system, the major decisions on production must be made by the firms. All of the major production decisions in a modern economy involve the use of capital goods. An economic system in which the state controls capital would lead to state domination of the economy. Such a system would be a variant of state socialism.

What advantages does a market socialist economy have over capitalism (besides the fact that, in the absence of capitalists, there is no problem of capitalist exploitation)? According to Jon Elster, a principal answer stems from the issues of decision-making and creative work.[4]

Few people like to take orders from others, especially in significant areas of life. Under capitalism, the employer tells workers what they must produce and how they are to do it. Although many modern firms encourage workers' suggestions and respond to their grievances, workers generally have little ultimate influence over production decisions. In cooperatives, the situation is quite different. There, workers themselves make the key decisions. Clearly, according to Elster, market socialism has a decisive advantage in this area over free-market capitalism.

Elster's argument rests on an unsupported assumption. He takes for granted that workers (and capitalists, for that matter) have a great deal of freedom of choice in reaching decisions about production. In a sense, they do: if, for example, a cooperative engaged in auto manufacture decides to abolish assembly lines and require of its members no more than a three-hour working day, nothing will stop these decisions from being carried out. The workers, by hypothesis, own the firm; they are legally free to produce as they please.

It is a safe bet, however, that a firm making these decisions would soon find itself out of business and its owners unemployed. Since cooperatives are in competition with one another for the cash of consumers in the same fashion as capitalist firms, they must conform to a rigid imperative: make sufficient profit to stay in business, or go under. The entire point of relying on the market to solve the calculation problem is that each firm, by looking at the estimated costs and profits of various alternatives, can determine what to do *without* extensive indecision. If firms generally decided to go their own way in spite of the signals of the market, there would be no economic system at all. A system in which the various cooperatives do *not* respond to the market, but make production decisions by arguments among themselves, is *not* market socialism. Practically no one—certainly not the analytical Marxists—recommends this sort of syndicalism.

An objection might be raised here. Although a cooperative firm cannot sustain protracted losses and survive, it may be that there are several alternative methods of production available that allow it to make a profit. A capitalist firm in a situation of this kind will tend to pursue the highest possible profit. Usually its *raison d'être* is to make as much money as possible.

A cooperative need not accept so rigid a restriction; its owners can decide on the profitable policy that best suits their needs. If, for example, workers do not wish to exert themselves to the maximum extent feasible, they are perfectly in order if they decide on some less taxing alternative—provided that they make a profit.

This objection has force only in the unlikely event that all firms that confront two or more alternatives practically always choose a less demanding course of action, rather than the more profitable one. If a significant minority of firms chooses the more profitable alternative, the firms that constitute this group will have a competitive advantage over their less mercenary rivals. They will tend gradually to supplant their rivals that are less profit-oriented. Thus, the conclusion of our argument still stands against this objection: a firm that operates on the market, whether owned by a capitalist or by workers, lacks the room for maneuver which Elster's argument presupposes. There is of course the possibility that a less demanding course of action is also the most profitable. But if this were the case, a capitalist firm would also adopt it; the cooperative has no special point in its favor.

Elster's argument seems open to objection on other grounds. Is it obvious that people do like to decide as a group the conditions under which they work, rather than accept a labor contract from an employer? It is probably true that each person likes to decide such matters for himself, rather than accept orders from others. But this preferred state of affairs will not occur in a cooperative.

No cooperative permits each worker to decide for himself the conditions under which he is to labor. Rather, the entire group of worker-owners makes production decisions jointly, voting with equal (or close to equal) weight. An individual worker seems little more at liberty to set his own conditions of labor than he is as an employee of a capitalist.

Defenders of cooperatives will admit that this is true, but reply that in a cooperative he at least has a vote: further, he can make himself heard at meetings in which the votes are cast. This is true enough; on the other hand, though, many people find the pettiness and bickering which frequently accompany such meetings less than edifying. In addition, meetings take up considerable time; they are often dominated by those who are more skilled at building coalitions, better in debate, better able to wait out those with opposing views, etc. Equal shares by no means implies equal voices in the decisions leading to policies. If workers do not like having decisions about their job made for them, they are unlikely to find cooperatives suitable to their purposes.

Perhaps Elster would reply that the very process of debate just discussed brings enjoyment to those who participate in it. No doubt some may find this to be true, but others definitely do not. Though it is hardly conclusive evidence, most academics tend to dislike department meetings, even though they often settle important questions of policy. Also, time spent in meetings is a cost of production; firms that spend long hours in board meetings will be at a competitive disadvantage, compared to firms whose workers dispose of problems quickly.

There is yet another objection to be made to Elster's argument. Is it in fact the case that workers for capitalist firms have little or no influence over their working conditions? One might at first glance think that it is obvious that they do not: most workers, as already mentioned, labor under the terms set by their employer. This superficially plausible view disregards a basic principle of buying and selling on the free market.

Suppose that someone wishes to exchange his apples for someone else's oranges. The two parties to the exchange bargain; they arrive at an exchange rate of one apple for one orange. So far, it is apparent that (other things being equal) neither party is subject to the other's direction. Both have agreed to a voluntary exchange.

Imagine that the situation is slightly varied. The orange seller posts a sign stating that he will exchange oranges for apples at a ratio of one to one. Is it the case that the owner of apples, formerly equal in autonomy to his trading partner, now stands under the latter's command?

It hardly seems so. Each party is free, just as before, to make the exchange or refuse to do so. If the apple owner does not like the posted rate, he remains at liberty to offer a different price or to exchange with someone else. In general, the fact that an exchange takes place by one party who accepts or refuses an offer made by another instead of bargaining makes little difference.

The qualification 'in general' is needed because of the following possibility. Even though a stated price does not preclude bargaining, it may turn out that someone's ability to set the price which the parties initially face gives him an advantage. The person who wishes a different price must do something: the price-setter has the advantage that those who wish to avoid the transaction costs of bargaining can do so simply by accepting the given price.

Further, it is sometimes the case that bargainers have little information on which to base their offers. The very fact that someone has made a definite proposal by posting a price may suffice to make that price a natural point of agreement between bargainers who are otherwise uncertain what to do.

But these qualifications, it seems to me, do not amount to very much. Someone who posted a price that others found unacceptable would quickly discover that the transactions costs mentioned above pose only a paper-thin barrier to those dissatisfied. Experience will readily overturn whatever advantages a posted price has as a natural point of agreement, if it transpires that the agreement operates to the disadvantage of the price-taker.

Applied to labor bargains, the lesson of the examples presented above is obvious. Even though job offers are usually by owners who offer terms that workers must accept or reject, this does not detract from the freedom of the workers. The capitalist who offers terms that workers find unacceptable will find himself outbid by employers who make better offers. *Prima facie,* there seems no reason to make an exception to the conclusions reached above about exchange in this case. Why are wage bargains different?

Of course, one can advance special hypotheses in which workers do face a disadvantage. A favorite among Marxists is that an agreement among large employers keeps down wages by the maintenance of a "reserve army of the unemployed." The problems of this hypothesis do not require extended treatment here, since analytic Marxists have not adopted it. Suffice it to say that this theory appears questionable: if there are unemployed workers, does this not suggest high wages rather than low?

Even if this problem in the theory could be overcome, and empirical evidence were offered in the theory's support, one would still need to show that capitalism was intrinsically liable to produce a "reserve army." The existence of such a class might be a historical accident, rather than something the characteristics of capitalism made necessary or even likely. As the analytic Marxists do not hypothesize this phenomenon, all this is by the way.

To sum up the argument so far: Elster's contention that cooperatives offer workers greater scope over decision-making than do capitalist firms ought to be rejected. In a market economy, *neither* type of firm has *that* much autonomy over basic decisions of production. The fact that capitalists usually set the terms of employment in advance does not by itself make workers less free to bargain over these terms. Even if workers in cooperatives *did* have a larger role in business decisions than those employed by capitalists, whether this creates much of an advantage for cooperatives is doubtful. How much good to each worker is the right to cast a ballot on his working conditions? There is a parallel here with democratic political elections. In the United States and other countries, voter turnout is often low. So-called voter apathy may reflect a correct perception of the limited effectiveness of votes in affecting policies that appear determined by external conditions.

Elster has another string in his bow. Basing himself on various psychological studies, he contends that human beings need creative work in order to be happy. He contends, further, that this need outranks the desire for a high income. Capitalism gives precedence to the wrong item: a market socialist system allows creativity its proper role.

Here we can be relatively brief, since to strike at this argument requires only that we question its last sentence. There is no need to challenge the desirability of creative work, since Elster gives us no reason that is independent of his previous argument to think that work is more likely to be creative under a market socialist system than under capitalism. If his argument is that workers in cooperatives can decide to work in a more creative fashion, whereas they lack this freedom under capitalist employment, this presupposes his earlier contention of greater workers' freedom of decision in cooperatives. If, as contended earlier, that argument fails, his present thesis must also be dismissed. Further, workers under capitalism who are especially creative are free to form their own businesses. Under cooperative socialism, workers wishing to form a new business would have to establish a new cooperative. This seems a difficult task, since the members of the new cooperative might lose their ownership shares of the cooperatives in which they formerly worked.

Elster might attempt the following rejoinder. Even if workers find it difficult to secure conditions for creative work under either capitalism or market socialism, this nevertheless remains essential for their happiness. The state must therefore enter the scene and regulate matters so that workers do not face inexorable pressure to earn as much money as possible.

But Elster himself declines to follow this path. As he notes, this course of action would involve the state in a grossly paternalistic policy. People do not know what is best for them; the state must therefore step in and require them to work creatively. It hardly seems conducive to happiness to ram creativity down people's throats, whether they wish it or not.

Even if the overwhelming majority of people favor working conditions of the type Elster deems creative, the case for state intervention has not been made. If people did have this preference, what would prevent them from getting the terms they wish in their wage contracts? This point, incidentally, does not contradict the contention made earlier that cooperatives, like capitalist firms, would be driven to pursue profit. Here we assume that workers who desire creative work require less in wages than they otherwise would. There is thus no loss to the firm; no obstacle confronts it in its drive for profit. Given the appropriate preferences of workers, both capitalist and cooperative firms can supply the working conditions the laborers desire.

In fact, workers in the free market do act (in part) in just the way suggested. Many workers in modern developed economies work under pleasant conditions, get paid vacations and health plans, etc. *All* benefits that a worker receives form part of wages; it is not the case that workers inexorably pursue money and nothing else.

Of course, the benefits workers characteristically receive in modern capitalist economies do not, for Elster, suffice to constitute creative work: otherwise, he would not have criticized capitalism. But even if one agrees with Elster that working conditions in capitalism lack creativity, no significant criticism of capitalism follows from this. Creativity is only one of several goods that people may find attractive; trade-offs among goods prevent any one of these from being attained to the maximum degree.

But what of Elster's basic contention? If creative work is necessary for happiness, does not what we have said so far imply that workers *must* be unhappy? Neither capitalism nor market socialism is likely to provide the conditions Elster thinks are required for happiness.

Fortunately, the situation is not this bleak. So far, there has been a glaring gap in our discussion of Elster's argument. We have referred indifferently to creativity and creative *work*. But these are by no means the same, if 'work' is understood as 'gainful employment'. Why *must* people fulfill their needs for creative activities in their job? People in boring, non-creative jobs often have hobbies or derive satisfaction from (for example) raising a family. It certainly does not follow from the need for creative work that people need creativity in their *jobs*. Elster's argument rests on an ambiguity in the term 'work'. It can mean either 'activity' or 'livelihood'. Elster offers no reason for thinking that one must have a creative livelihood in order to be happy.

In fact, some people like boring, repetitive work or work that calls for little in the way of responsibility. People in such jobs have nothing to worry about when they go home—a state of affairs that academics who cannot get their minds off their subjects may envy. What, one must wonder, is boring work? Many workers—for example, auto mechanics and skilled laborers—do work that requires creativity and independence, however little their activities appeal to some academics.

There is also another problem with Elster's argument. He claims that people need creative work in order to be happy. No definition of 'creative work' has been offered here: we have assumed that it has a common-sense meaning that need not be explicitly spelled out. However one might choose to define creative work, one thing should be clear: the conditions that are most favorable to creative work are not the same as the creative work itself.

Elster may be right that creative work is necessary for happiness. But the measures he suggests—that is, changes in the circumstances of work—will, if he is right, at best increase the chances for some people to be happy. That is to say, Elster maintains that creative work is a necessary condition for happiness; certain working conditions make creative work more likely; and market socialism makes these conditions easier to achieve than under capitalism. What if the conditions Elster favors do not suffice to make most people creative enough to be happy?

Turning from Elster, I now want to show that it is entirely rational for workers to prefer capitalist employment to participation in cooperatives. Perhaps the most readily apparent reason controverts a commonly claimed advantage of this form of organization.

Unlike those who work for capitalists, laborers who form cooperatives do not receive their remuneration in wages. Instead, they receive whatever profits the firm makes; after all, they own the firm. Is it not more desirable that workers receive all profits than that they be limited to fixed wages, while all profit goes to capitalists?

No doubt workers prefer getting as much money as they can; however, if in a cooperative system they receive profits if a firm does well, they will confront losses if the firm does poorly. It is hardly reasonable to think that workers would, as a rule, be willing to place at risk the funds they require to secure the essential goods required for living. Workers under capitalism can transfer this risk to the entrepreneur. Unless a capitalist firm collapses, the workers employed by it will receive the wages for which they have contracted. Surely it is a major advantage of capitalism that workers do not have to bear the risk of getting little or nothing.

This argument does *not* depend on the assumption that workers are more risk-averse than capitalists. The conclusion still follows even if everyone has exactly the same risk-preference. Someone's willingness to assume risk usually does not remain constant regardless of income and wealth possessed. Generally, if one has more money, one is more willing to assume risk than if one's worth is low. Thus, even if workers in the actual world are unwilling to accept much risk, this does *not* imply different preferences from those of entrepreneurs. It might be the case both that if workers had more funds, they would be willing to engage in risky enterprises and that if capitalists lacked funds, they would be risk-averse. The preference for risk of the two groups might be exactly alike; since workers usually have less accumulated funds than capitalists, however, workers may in the actual world be more risk-averse.

Of course, if workers are more risk-averse than capitalists, the argument is all the stronger. Each group is able in a capitalist economy to secure the satisfaction of its respective preference for risk. In a regime of cooperatives, this is not the case. The workers have to bear all the risk themselves.

It would be a most inadequate response to this argument to say that in a market socialist order workers will have more money and hence be willing to bear risk. *Why* will workers be better off in this system? The response just suggested begs completely the principal question at issue in our discussion: which system is, in fact, the better one?

A more adequate response might be the following. In a regime that consisted only of cooperatives, the point just raised might be correct. In a market socialist regime, however, matters are different. The state can step in and cushion the fall of those who lose out because of business failure. Thus, with this system we can have the best of both possible worlds. Workers who belong to cooperatives that make a profit will be better off than they would have been under capitalism. The others, by having their losses cushioned, can do just as well.

This suggested answer also fails. The very point of market socialism, as opposed to the centralized kind, is that it allegedly can deal with the calculation difficulties adumbrated by Mises. The proposed cushioning brings back precisely the problem from which market socialism was supposed to be the solution, since it redistributes the profits and losses that, under market socialism, guide the firms to as close a semblance of the free market as possible. If a cooperative firm's losses are not allowed to bite into the wages of its workers to any significant extent, inefficient firms will not be at a competitive disadvantage.

Even firms that do well in a cooperative system will still rank as inefficient by the standards of the free market. If a business is successful and expands, it will sometimes have a choice between methods of production that are capital-intensive or labor-intensive. A foundry, for example, might increase production either by adding increased machines for casting or by hiring new employees.

In the capitalist market, the entrepreneur will resolve choices of this sort by asking which technique offers the greater expectation of profit. Those who decide correctly will tend to supplant less successful forecasters; there is thus a tendency toward the use of the most efficient feasible method of production.

Cooperatives also confront the demands of efficiency. If the correct option is a capital-intensive technique, the firm can proceed in the same fashion as a capitalist firm. With labor-intensive production methods, a decisive difference between the two economic systems arises.

A cooperative is owned by those who work in it. If additional labor is hired, the new recruits join not only as workers but as owners as well. They are then entitled to their share of the firm's profits. Their shares, as equal owners, consist of the appropriate parts of the total proceeds of the firm: their gain is not confined to a share of the revenue their contribution adds to the firm. Further, since an owner is on board permanently, new workers will continue to receive shares of revenue so long as the firm stays in operation.

The consequences are clear. Cooperative firms will hire new workers only if their lifetime contribution is expected to raise the revenue of each existing worker-owner. A new worker, in other words, must bring a permanent advantage to present workers to justify his employment.[5]

A capitalist entrepreneur confronts much less stringent requirements. He can hire new workers as long as what they add to the firm's output is worth more than what he pays them. In the language of economics, new workers can be hired so long as the marginal revenue their employment enables the firm to obtain exceeds the marginal cost their hiring entails. (This includes their wages as well as costs resulting from their use of the firm's capital goods, etc.)

Cooperative firms will therefore tend to be inefficient as compared with capitalist firms, whenever labor-intensive techniques are the most efficient method of increasing production. Thus, even workers who anticipate success in an economic system composed of cooperative firms will find it rational to hesitate before embracing this alternative to capitalism. Those less optimistic about their prospects, of course, have even greater reason for aversion to cooperatives. Expected losses have little motivational force.

One objection to this argument is that the correct conclusion from the line of reasoning just advanced is the opposite of what we have indicated. Capital-intensive techniques add to productivity: this, after all, is the principle of the Industrial Revolution. Cooperative firms will tend to be *more* efficient than capitalist firms. This counterargument rests on a false assumption. It is correct, of course, that the extensive use of machinery is vastly more productive than unaided human labor. It does not follow from this that in any choice between a capital-intensive and a labor-intensive technique, the former is always more efficient. In the absence of some reason for thinking that capitalist entrepreneurs systematically underestimate the efficiency of capital-intensive production methods, this argument fails.[6]

The point just given leads to an even more serious difficulty for cooperative firms. Because of the problems in hiring new workers, cooperative regimes would have a strong tendency to lock employees into one firm. Labor mobility would be substantially less than under capitalism.

The severe problem just referred to is *not* the loss of economic efficiency, bad enough as this is. Rather, the problem is this: in the event a cooperative firm went out of business, what would happen to its workers? Since, by definition, most workers are not above-average in their productivity, why would new firms hire them? The owners of successful firms would drag down their own incomes if they did so.

The problems confronting those of below-average productivity would be worse still. Who would want them on board? If workers of low productivity are allowed to join a cooperative, what could be done if they seriously interfere with the operations of the business? They cannot easily be fired, since they are part owners of the business. To fire someone, he must be bought out. The problem of replacing inefficient labor makes cooperatives less adaptable and more likely to fail than capitalist firms. Further, what would happen as new generations of workers entered the labor market? What if existing firms hired only an elite few from each new generation? Who would provide for the rest? (I assume for the sake of argument that, at the starting point of the system, everyone is employed.)

These difficulties suggest that an economic system composed entirely of cooperative firms would have grave difficulty functioning. Anyone who realized this would have a reason of compelling significance to avoid a society of this type.

It is a safe bet that the advocates of market socialism will here seek refuge in the state. Cooperatives will not be permitted to act entirely as their owners please, as far as the employment of new workers is concerned. The state will step in and solve the difficulties we have raised.

If the state interferes with the operation of the cooperative firms, another problem arises. This requires only very brief mention, since it has been discussed already in another context. A market socialist system is supposed to solve the problem of economic calculation by means of non-capitalist market prices. To the extent the state blocks the market and replaces it with central direction, it confronts anew the calculation problem.

One final difficulty for a cooperative economy rests in the division of labor. As everyone who has so much as glanced at Adam Smith's *The Wealth of Nations* knows, the division of labor has been responsible for vast increases in productivity. As a rule of thumb, whatever promotes the division of labor enhances economic efficiency; whatever places obstacles in its path impedes efficiency.

In a capitalist economy, the chief risk-takers in business are the entrepreneurs. Not only do they take the burden of risk from their employees, as explained at the start of the present discussion; they also become specialists in risk-taking. In a cooperative, by contrast, the owners are workers as well. Specialization cannot develop in risk-taking to as great an extent as under capitalism. Here, then, is yet another reason for those interested in economic productivity to steer clear of cooperatives. A cooperative can, of course, have employees who manage the firm, but they will not have full powers of decision. If they do, the cooperative has transformed itself into a capitalist firm. Thus, even cooperatives with full-time managers will not carry specialization in risk-taking as far as capitalist firms.

The conclusion of this part of our discussion will hardly come as a surprise. Cooperatives often compel people to take risks they prefer to avoid. They tend to be inefficient as compared with capitalist firms, even if they are successful whenever labor-intensive techniques of production are better suited to expanding production than capital-intensive techniques. They make it difficult to change jobs, and threaten many with permanent unemployment. They impede the growth of specialization in risk-taking. Resort to the state to solve these problems will, by impeding the operation of the market, dissipate the ability of a market socialist order to solve Mises's calculation problem. For these reasons, and contrary to the views of several of the analytical Marxists, most people will find it eminently rational *not* to enlist as recruits to a cooperative commonwealth.

Suppose that every consideration we have thus far advanced against cooperatives is wrong. Even so, I suspect that workers will still find a capitalist economy preferable to the market socialist alternative. Why? In a free-market economy, people who wish to form cooperatives are at liberty to do so. In a market socialist system, those who prefer capitalist employment are *not* free to obtain what they wish. This, at any rate, is the way the advocates of a market socialist order composed of cooperatives have characterized their system. If "capitalist acts between consenting adults" were allowed, then the system qualifies as a free-market regime.

The advocates of the capitalist free market will interpose no force against people, even if the vast majority of people prefer cooperatives. But is this outcome likely to occur? Only a minority of workers in modern capitalist economies join cooperatives. This is true in spite of the fact that in some instances (for example, in Britain and Israel), the cooperative movement is well-established and in command of substantial assets. Further, as Robert Nozick has noted, substantial social prestige results for Israelis who join *kibbutzim* (cooperatively owned farms), as these institutions are very favorably portrayed in the Israeli educational system. Yet the prestige has not been sufficient to attract most Israeli citizens to this form of life. Membership in Israeli cooperatives has never exceeded about five percent of the population.[7] *Kibbutzim* in recent years have also tended to introduce capitalist features—for example, more privacy and greater ability to attain individual wealth.

An advocate of market socialism might respond: if it is true that in a capitalist system comparatively few workers wish to join cooperatives, things would be different if the entire economy consisted of cooperative firms. It does not follow from the fact that people are reluctant to join islands of cooperatives in a sea of capitalist firms that they do not wish a market socialism regime of cooperatives.

True enough, this does not follow logically. But we have at least *some* reason for thinking that most workers view cooperatives with less than complete enthusiasm. Why is it the case that matters are different if the choice is that of a society that is predominantly cooperative rather than capitalist? Further, if most workers do choose to join cooperatives, that just *is* a choice for a *society* of cooperatives, provided that most people who join them are aware that the majority of workers are also acting in this way.

Considerable historical evidence exists to show that agricultural workers are extremely averse to joining cooperatives. Most notoriously, the Soviet collectivization of the 1930s brought about the deaths of millions of people. Estimates of "excess deaths" in Soviet Russia from 1929–1936 range from 8 million to 15.2 million people.[8]

This disastrous Soviet venture does not stand alone. Workers and peasants in Communist countries have manifested extreme aversion to collectivization. Efforts to collectivize peasants in the Baltic Republics and Poland in the later 1940s and early 1950s met with massive resistance. This was quashed forcibly, and many workers were deported.[9] Similarly, the much praised Yugoslavian cooperatives have shown "a continued failure to implement adequate labor incentives for farm workers."[10]

Perhaps the best market socialist response to the argument that workers have demonstrated in action their reluctance to join cooperatives is the following. (Even this socialist response, it should be noted, fails to address problems of aversion to cooperatives by workers in socialist societies.) Although workers in a capitalist society are legally at liberty to join cooperatives, in practice very difficult obstacles confront those who wish to leave the capitalist market. It is unfair, then, to judge the desirability of a market socialist society by asking how many workers in an existing capitalist society are willing to enter cooperatives.

What is the nature of these difficulties? Some depend on controversial assumptions about the way a capitalist society works.[11] G. A. Cohen suggests, for example, that the capitalist state would use force if 'too many' workers wanted to leave the capitalist market. It is sometimes claimed that banks are reluctant to lend money to cooperatives. Bankers wish to retain an economic system in which they exercise great power and will do what they can to bar the way to changes that threaten their interests.

These claims will not be assessed in detail here. To do so would necessitate a great deal of empirical investigation; although some of the analytical Marxists have advanced claims of this kind, they have not advanced arguments supporting these conjectures. As suggested in our discussion of Cohen in a preceding chapter, it is a large step from "market socialism is more desirable than capitalism for workers if one assumes as true a particular account for the way capitalist society works" to "Market socialism is more desirable than capitalism for workers." The assumptions behind such an account need not be of a distinctively Marxist kind. But whether Marxist or not, anti-capitalist assumptions require arguments in their favor to justify their adoption.

Of course, so do pro-capitalist assumptions, and I have not done the empirical work required to confirm or refute them. All that is being attempted here is to sketch the logical structure of the argument over cooperatives.

A more theoretically important argument that workers in capitalism cannot readily form cooperatives has been offered by David Miller.[12] Miller's objection is free from the weakness of assuming as given controversial assumptions about capitalist society.

Miller thinks that even if the vast majority of workers prefer a market socialist economy to a capitalist one, this preference may be unrealizable if one starts from a capitalist economy. Workers, especially those of outstanding ability, may find that they can earn more wages in existing capitalist firms than in cooperatives. Confronted with the choice of working for a capitalist firm or joining a cooperative, even those workers who want cooperatives will be reluctant to leave the capitalist firms that employ them.

Why should they? No matter how much they may want a non-capitalist society, nothing that any individual can do will have a significant effect in determining the issues. What is one vote among millions? It is therefore rational for an advocate of cooperatives who can earn more wages in capitalist employment to follow the path of least resistance and accept the higher wages. In brief, Miller contends that supporters of cooperatives face a Prisoner's Dilemma. Even if, by their own lights, everyone would would be better off in a market socialist system, it will be rational for each person who can individually gain from doing so to accept capitalist employment. The result will be the continuance of capitalism, contrary by hypothesis to the wishes of the vast majority.

Miller has not made out his case. He presents no argument that the structure of preferences must fulfill the requirements of a Prisoner's Dilemma. What if, instead, many of those who want a market socialist society would benefit from joining cooperatives in a capitalist society as well? In this event, no Prisoner's Dilemma would exist: working for a capitalist would not dominate joining a cooperative. In the language of game theory, an Assurance Game would result. Very roughly, this is a situation where people agree on what outcome is best (both individually and collectively) but face coordination problems. No doubt, as Elster has pointed out, Assurance Games pose coordination problems of their own. But there is nothing *irrational* in these circumstances about an agreement to establish a workers' cooperative under capitalism. (I do not mean that it is rational to attempt this: it is only that an agreement to do so adds no *new* irrationality.) As to the coordination problems of an Assurance Game, no one said things have to be easy. Once more, though, I have not shown that Miller is *in fact* wrong; I have attempted to show only that no proof has been given that workers face a Prisoner's Dilemma of the type Miller discusses.

The conclusions critical of market socialism which have been advanced in this chapter stand under a cloud. At the beginning of the discussion, we assumed (just for the purpose of argument) that capitalist employment is exploitative. On this assumption, it appears that one cannot claim that a conclusive argument has been advanced against market socialism, even if all the points we have raised against it are telling. Should we then weigh the disadvantages of cooperatives against the injustice of capitalist exploitation?

If the case I have endeavored to make against market socialism is essentially correct, the answer to the question just posed is "no." The best argument that capitalist employment involves exploitation is the collective unfreedom argument of G. A. Cohen, analyzed in the preceding chapter. (Here 'exploitation' is used in a very wide sense. Roughly, it means anything morally undesirable about employment relations under capitalism.)

His argument depends on the assumption that workers cannot leave the proletariat *en masse*. But his discussion took the alternative to capitalist employment to be the formation of small businesses. He did not discuss in detail the formation of cooperatives. But unless it can be shown that workers in a capitalist economy are not free to form cooperatives, then it is *false* that the proletariat under capitalism is collectively unfree. Since Cohen's argument fails, and it is the strongest argument that capitalist employment of labor is exploitative, our temporary concession can be withdrawn. To the extent that the analytical Marxist case against capitalism rests upon the superiority of market socialism, it ought to be rejected.

Conclusion

Analytical Marxism is a movement that has arisen in response to the theoretical difficulties of standard Marxism and the less-than-ideal record of existing socialist governments. The members of the group, principally G. A. Cohen, Jon Elster, and John Roemer, propose to solve the theoretical problems of Marxism through reconstructing key elements of that theory by means of analytical philosophy and modern economics. What they cannot reconstruct, they toss overboard. They have addressed the practical problems of an alternative to capitalism in less detail; to the extent they have done so, most of them support a market socialist economy consisting of cooperatively-owned firms.

The principal task of this book has been to assess the analytical Marxist criticism of free-market capitalism. Marx himself portrayed capitalism as a system whose "secret" lay in the exploitation of the proletariat by capitalists. The analytical Marxists agree with Marx that capitalism is exploitative. They have, however, completely undermined the basis of Marx's claim: his labor theory of value.

Why, then, do they continue to insist that capitalism is exploitative? Two different (though compatible) responses have emerged from the group. Roemer has introduced a new concept of exploitation that does not depend on the labor theory of value. However, he fails entirely to show that there is anything objectionable in the existence of his sort of exploitation, unless one accepts that equality of wealth and income or some other non-market rule of distribution is required by morality. It is entirely possible on Roemer's account for workers to exploit capitalists, hardly a characteristically Marxist view.

Cohen contends that workers are collectively unfree to leave the proletariat. His argument, while stronger than Roemer's, also ought to be rejected. Workers under capitalism *are* collectively free to exit the proleteriat.

Cohen's work on the justice of capitalism has not been confined to the topic of workers' freedom. He has also sought to refute arguments that people have individual moral rights to own property. The libertarian arguments that Cohen criticizes are mainly those advanced by Robert Nozick. The objections that Cohen raises to natural rights arguments in defense of property rights do not work.

Finally, the alternative to capitalism most in favor among the analytical Marxists—that is, market socialism—is very far from being superior to free market capitalism. It is likely that most workers would find it rational to avoid an economic system that consisted mainly of cooperative firms.

Analytical Marxism—though often raising issues of great intrinsic interest—must, so far as its indictment of capitalism is concerned, be dismissed as a complete failure. The movement is analytical, but not analytical enough.

Notes

Chapter 1

1. The difference between labor and labor power, and the way in which this difference results in profit, is a standard feature of nearly all interpretations of classical Marxism. See, e.g., John Roemer, *Analytical Foundations of Marxian Economic Theory* (Cambridge: Cambridge University Press, 1981).
2. Jon Elster, *Making Sense of Marx* (Cambridge University Press, 1985), argues strongly for the view that Marx does not assume an inevitable succession of stages. An earlier work, ignored by most of the recent literature, that takes a similar view is Karl-August Wittfogel, *Oriental Despotism* (New Haven: Yale University Press, 1957). Wittfogel uses Marx's concept of Oriental despotism to analyze contemporary Soviet Communism.
3. Marx's praise for the productivity of capitalism has sometimes been cited by anti-socialist writers, e.g., Max Eastman, *Reflections on the Failure of Socialism* (New York: Devin-Adair, 1955).
4. This point is used as a main argument by writers who deny that Marx had a theory of justice. See, e.g., Allen Wood, *Karl Marx* (London: Routledge, 1981). Although Wood is a noted philosopher, I do not consider his work in detail here, as he is too uncritical of Marx to count as a member of the analytic school.
5. As suggested in the text, the question of Marx's attitude toward the justice of capitalism has aroused great controversy. A good entry into the controversy is a volume of reprints from *Philosophy and Public Affairs* entitled *Marx and Justice*. Also, Steven Lukes, *Marxism and Morality* (Oxford: Oxford University Press, 1985) offers a succinct and accurate summary of the controversy. Further references may be found in the comprehensive notes of Norman Geras, *Literature of Revolution* (London: Verso, 1986).
6. The best short presentation of the positive interpretation of the Industrial Revolution is F. A. Hayek, ed., *Capitalism and the Historians* (Chicago: University of Chicago, 1954).
7. See, e.g., his bitter pamphlet, *The Proletarian Revolution and the Renegade Kautsky*.
8. The later work, Paul Baran and Paul Sweezy, *Monopoly Capital* (New York: Monthly Review Press, 1966) makes Sweezy's Keynesianism even more obvious than before.

9. I state the theory in this way here rather in the counterfactual way given earlier because Böhm-Bawerk took the theory in the fashion stated in this paragraph.
10. The mathematical flaw is tersely stated in Elster, *Making Sense of Marx*.
11. I have discussed these figures in *Critics of Marxism* (New Brunswick: Transaction, 1986).
12. Popper never accepted the so-called verifiability criterion of meaning and has always distanced himself from the Vienna Circle and other logical positivists.
13. Sidney Hook first attracted wide attention in the period 1929–1932 with the publication of two books: *Toward the Understanding of Karl Marx* and *From Hegel to Marx*. The former blended the teachings of Marx with the pragmatist views of his philosophical mentor at Columbia, John Dewey. Though at one time ardently courted by the Communist Party, he had broken with Moscow by the early 1930s. Since that time, he has been one of the foremost American opponents of Communism. He retains a belief in "social democracy," as he terms it: to what extent this involves belief in socialism is unclear. He strongly opposes the view of Kolakowski that Leninism accurately reflects the dictatorial propensity of Marxism.
14. Compare the strained effort of the Anglo-Indian Communist R. Palme Dutt, *Problems of Contemporary History* (London: Lawrence & Wishart, 1963), to argue that Marx really was right after all: he *did* expect the revolution first to occur in Russia. Dutt relies on Marx's *obiter dicta* in a few letters to Russian revolutionaries.
15. A better-than-average sample of the work of this school is Maurice Cornforth, *The Open Philosophy and the Open Society* (New York: International Publishers, 1968). Its arguments are very weak and take for granted the truth of Marxism.
16. See the remarks on this point in J. M. E. McTaggart, *Studies in the Hegelian Dialectic* (Cambridge, 1898).
17. Jon Elster, *Making Sense of Marx*, p. 120.

Chapter 2

1. Also, this definition ensures against an easy but irrelevant counterexample to the claim that capitalism rests on exploitation. In a one-person "Crusoe" economy everything is privately owned, but no exploitation of the lone resident by himself is possible. But presumably a Crusoe economy (unless Crusoe is Superman) will not be highly developed.
2. See the brief but penetrating remarks on this point by Ludwig von Mises, *Socialism* (New Haven: Yale University Press, 1951). A Marxist interpretation of fascism is contained in Franz Neumann, *Behemoth* (New York: Columbia University Press, 1944). Although contemporary Marxists such as Richard Miller look on this work with great favor, its view of

fascism as a tool of big business has been challenged by the research of Henry A. Turner and others.

3. Michael Polanyi and P. Craig Roberts are defenders of this view. It is strongly supported in David Ramsay Steele, *Marx and Mises* (Open Court: forthcoming). The classic source is Ludwig von Mises, *Socialism* (2nd edition; New Haven: Yale University Press, 1961).

4. John Rawls, *A Theory of Justice* (Cambridge: Harvard University Press, 1971), pp. 5, 62ff.

5. Some analytic Marxists, however (such as Robert Brenner), do attach enormous importance to the historical conditions that gave rise to capitalism.

6. The two most frequently discussed works are, of course, *A Theory of Justice* and Robert Nozick, *Anarchy, State, and Utopia* (New York: Basic Books, 1974).

7. Jon Elster, *Making Sense of Marx* (Cambridge: Cambridge University Press, 1985), p. 227.

8. Robert Nozick, "Coercion," ed. S. Morgenbesser, *Philosophy, Science, and Method: Essays in Honor of Ernest Nagel* (New York, 1969), pp. 440–72.

9. "The worker is neither bound to particular objects, nor to a particular manner of satisfaction. The sphere of his consumption is not qualitatively restricted." Karl Marx, *Grundrisse* (London: New Left Review, 1973), p. 283.

10. See F. A. von Hayek, et al., *Capitalism and the Historians* (Chicago, 1951). See in particular the essays of W. H. Hutt in this work. They subject to penetrating scrutiny the work of J. L. and Barbara Hammond, who maintained that the Industrial Revolution worsened the English workers' standard of living.

11. We shall endeavor to show in Chapter 5 that G. A. Cohen's analysis of proletarian collective unfreedom depends crucially on controversial Marxist assumptions of how capitalism works.

12. *Social Philosophy & Policy*, vol. 3, no. 2 (Spring 1986).

13. In his *One-Dimensional Man* (Boston: Beacon Press, 1966).

14. In fact, he does not present an argument of this type but instead analyzes various aspects of actually existing society, ranging from advertising to philosophy.

15. Jon Elster, *Making Sense of Marx* (Cambridge: Cambridge University Press, 1985), pp. 449–50.

16. Nozick, *Anarchy, State, and Utopia*, p. 163.

17. David Schweickart, *Capitalism or Worker Control?* (New York: Praeger, 1982). For further discussion, see my review in *International Philosophical Quarterly*, Vol. 26 (March 1986), pp. 96–98.

18. In another publication, I have set forward the argument for this point in much greater detail than is possible here. See my "Socialism, Dictatorship, and the Abolition of Rights," *Social Philosophy and Policy*, 1986.

19. For a description of such a proposal, see Jan Narveson, *The Libertarian Idea* (Philadelphia: Temple University Press, 1988), pp. 248–52.

20. This principle, which requires any change to benefit at least one person while making no one worse off, sets a requirement of what in welfare economics is called Pareto-superiority. If no change in the economy can move it to a superior position, the economy is Pareto-optimal. See Jules Coleman, *Markets, Morals, and the Law* (Cambridge: Cambridge University Press, 1988), p. 100.

21. In my view, little or no government action is required. See the penetrating discussion in Murray Rothbard, *Power and Market* (Menlo Park: Institute for Humane Studies, 1971). See also Ronald Coase, "The Problem of Social Cost," *Journal of Law and Economics,* vol. 3 (1960); James Buchanan, *The Limits of Liberty* (Chicago: University of Chicago Press, 1975), pp. 78, 82–83.

22. Karl Marx, *Wages, Price and Profit* (Peking: Foreign Languages Press, 1975), p. 146.

23. Both Cohen and Elster favor a Marxist theory of justice, but they admit that in supporting it they are going beyond Marx.

24. John Roemer, *A General Theory of Exploitation and Class* (Cambridge: Harvard University Press, 1982).

25. Steiner's views have been developed in a number of important papers. See, e.g., his "A Natural Right to the Means of Production," *Philosophical Quarterly,* 1974.

26. See Murray Rothbard, *Man, Economy, and State* (New York: Van Nostrand, 1962), vol. I, ch. 1.

27. See the discussion in F. A. Hayek, *Law, Legislation, and Liberty,* vol. II: *The Mirage of Social Justice.*

28. Here, "profit" is used in the Marxist sense to include interest and rent: it is not restricted to entrepreneurial profit.

Chapter 3

1. Another view of exploitation that does not involve the labor theory is discussed by G. A. Cohen in his "The Labor Theory of Value and the Concept of Exploitation," *Philosophy and Public Affairs,* 1979. Also, see Nancy Holstrom, "Exploitation," *Canadian Journal of Philosophy,* vol. 8 (Summer 1979), pp. 353–69.

2. Ian Steedman, *Marx after Sraffa* (London: New Left Books, 1977).

3. Pierro Sraffa, *Production of Commodities by Means of Commodities* (Cambridge: Cambridge University Press, 1963).

4. The position that Marx intends the labor theory as a hypothesis has been adopted by Thomas Sowell, *Marxism: Philosophy and Economics* (New York: William Morrow, 1985).

5. K. Marx, *Capital I* (New York: International Publishers, 1967), p. 37.

6. Elster, *Making Sense of Marx,* p. 140.

7. According to an unpublished paper cited by Elster, Ian Steedman contends this problem is even more acute if one takes into account wage differentials due to the unpleasantness of various kinds of labor. Elster, p. 131.

8. E. von Böhm-Bawerk, *Capital and Interest* (South Holland, Illinois: Libertarian Press, 1959), vol. II.
9. G. A. Cohen, "Marx's Dialectic of Labour," *Philosophy and Public Affairs,* Spring 1974.
10. Narveson's remarks regrettably cannot be cited, as they come from an unpublished paper which I do not now have at hand.
11. Cohen's analysis seems to rest on the assumption that labor creates all economic value. But why does it? Labor is only a factor of production, along with land and capital. Of course, on the Marxist theory of value, labor is indeed the source of value. But one cannot assume the truth of the labor theory of value in an argument ostensibly independent of it.

    However, there may be non-causal senses of explanation immune from this objection. Perhaps it would be better to say that it is not clear why *this* hypothetical will explain value.
12. I intend this point only as an objection to Marx's labor theory on the "hypothetical" reading. It does not show that all objective theories of value are wrong.
13. Rothbard, *Man, Economy, and State,* vol. I, ch. I.
14. Nozick, *Anarchy, State, and Utopia,* pp. 64–65.
15. One might adopt an objective value theory without the identity assumption, but no such theory has to my knowledge been constructed.
16. Elster, p. 193.
17. The easiest access to the controversy between Clark and Knight is George Stigler, *Production and Distribution Theories* (New York: Macmillan and Co., 1946). Clark's views are in his *The Distribution of Wealth* (New York: Macmillan, 1899). For Knight, see *Risk, Uncertainty, and Profit* (London: LSE, 1942).
18. Schweickart, ch. 1. See also N. Scott Arnold, "Capitalists and the Ethics of Contribution," *Canadian Journal of Philosophy,* vol. 15 (March 1985), pp. 87–102.
19. The most readily accessible presentation of Roemer's views is his *Free to Lose* (Cambridge: Harvard University Press, 1988). Roemer states there that exploitation "is said to exist if in a given economy some agents must work more time than is socially necessary . . . to earn their consumption bundles and others work less time than is socially necessary to earn their bundles" (p. 20). For the source of exploitation in inequality, see pp. 23ff.
20. ibid., pp. 76ff.
21. Virtually the whole of *Capital I* illustrates Marx's belief in the poor condition of the proletariat under capitalism.
22. Roemer, *Free to Lose,* pp. 96ff.
23. ibid., pp. 139ff.
24. ibid., p. 133.

Chapter 4

1. Cohen's criticisms of Nozick's theory of property will be found principally in two articles: "Nozick on Appropriation," *New Left Review,* no.

150 (1984), pp. 89–107, and "Self-Ownership, World-Ownership and Equality, Part II," *Social Philosophy & Policy,* vol. 3 (Spring 1986), no. 2, pp. 77–96.

2. Nozick, *Anarchy, State, and Utopia,* p. 178.
3. ibid., pp. 174–175.
4. Murray N. Rothbard, *The Ethics of Liberty* (Atlantic Highlands: Humanities Press, 1982), defends private property through appeal to self-ownership and Lockean labor mixture. Douglas Rasmussen and Douglas Den Uyl stress the necessity of property for human survival and flourishing. They both have contributions appearing in Tibor Machan, ed., *The Libertarian Reader* (Totowa: Rowan and Littlefield, 1982). Eric Mack defends the ethical egoist position that underlies the Den Uyl-Rasmussen argument: an article by Mack is included in the Machan volume. Ellen Frankel Paul, *Property Rights and Eminent Domain* (New Brunswick: Transaction Books, 1987), presents a comprehensive defense of the human survival and flourishing argument.
5. Cohen, "Self-Ownership," p. 82.
6. His failure to consider this point will be discussed later in this chapter.
7. Nozick, *Anarchy, State, and Utopia,* p. 178.
8. Perhaps I am being unfair to Cohen. He may be making an internal point against Nozick—that is, that on Nozick's own theory (though not necessarily on Cohen's), all physical objects begin unowned.
9. Cohen, "Self-Ownership," pp. 84–85. Dworkin's objection to theories of Steiner's type (though not specifically directed against Steiner) is in "What Is Equality? Part 2: Equality of Resources," *Philosophy and Public Affairs,* vol. 10 (1981), p. 322.
10. Cohen first introduced his "common-use" suggestion in "Capitalism, Freedom, and the Proletariat," in Alan Ryan, ed., *The Idea of Freedom* (Oxford: Oxford University Press, 1981).
11. Nozick, *Anarchy, State, and Utopia,* p. 151.
12. The term "closest instantiated realization" comes from Robert Nozick, *Philosophical Explanations* (Cambridge: Harvard University Press, 1981), pp. 51ff. The interpretation of the proviso I suggest here has against it Nozick's statement: "I assume that any adequate theory of justice in acquisition will contain a proviso similar to the weaker of the ones we have attributed to Locke" (*Anarchy, State, and Utopia,* p. 178). I base the suggestion on conversations with Nozick in 1981.
13. *Anarchy, State, and Utopia,* p. 175.
14. Eduard von Hartmann was a late nineteenth-century disciple of Schopenhauer. His most influential work is *The Philosophy of the Unconscious.* Like Schopenhauer, he thought the cessation of willing was desirable. If this took place, the human race would end.
15. *Anarchy, State, and Utopia,* pp. 161–63.
16. Cohen's criticisms of the example are in "Robert Nozick and Wilt Chamberlain," in John Arthur and William Shaw, eds., *Justice and Economic Distribution* (Englewood Cliffs, 1978).
17. Because Roemer is discussed only briefly here, I do not repeat the references to his works, which can be found in the preceding chapter.

Chapter 5

1. G. A. Cohen, "The Structure of Proletarian Unfreedom," ed. John Roemer, *Analytical Marxism* (Cambridge: Cambridge University Press, 1986), pp. 237–59.
2. ibid., p. 240.
3. ibid., p. 240.
4. ibid., p. 242. The only support offered for this is a quote from Marx.
5. John Gray, "Against Cohen on Proletarian Unfreedom," *Social Philosophy and Policy*, vol. 6, no. 1 (Fall 1988), pp. 77–112, has criticized Cohen principally on the grounds that his case of collective unfreedom is unimportant.
6. Cohen, "Structure of Unfreedom," p. 245. Cohen states that "although, in a collective sense, workers are forced to sell their labour-power, scarcely any particular proletarian is forced to sell himself even to some capitalist or other." This implies that selling one's labour-power to a capitalist is selling part of oneself.
7. Robert Nozick, *Anarchy, State, and Utopia* (New York: Basic Books, 1974), pp. 262–64.
8. Cohen, "Structure of Unfreedom," p. 238.
9. ibid., p. 250.
10. ibid., p. 241.
11. ibid., pp. 245–46.
12. Cohen himself recognizes this point: see the quotation given in note 6 above. However, he fails to see its full ramifications.
13. Cohen, "Structure of Unfreedom," p. 256.
14. ibid., p. 258.
15. G. A. Cohen, *Karl Marx's Theory of History: A Defence* (Princeton: Princeton University Press, 1978), pp. 309–12.

Chapter 6

1. John Roemer, *Free to Lose* (Cambridge: Harvard University Press, 1958), pp. 149–52. Richard Miller also seems more sympathetic than most other analytical Marxists to a centrally planned economy. He maintains that a centrally controlled economy can reduce inefficiencies present in capitalism, such as the existence of different brands of the same product. He states that his position receives support from the economic record of Soviet Russia.
2. Mises's 1920 article is available in English translation in F. A. Hayek, ed., *Collectivist Economic Planning* (London: Routledge and Sons, 1935), pp. 87-130. Much of it is incorporated into the fuller statement of Mises's case in *Socialism* (Indianapolis: Liberty Classics, 1981), pp. 135–36.
3. Oskar Lange and Fred M. Taylor, *On the Economic Theory of Socialism* (Minneapolis: University of Minnesota, 1938). Other important contri-

butions to the calculation controversy include T. J. B. Hoff, *Economic Calculation in the Socialist Society* (London: William Hodge, 1949) and F. A. Hayek, "Socialist Calculation III: The Competitive Solution," in *Individualism and the Economic Order* (Chicago: Henry Regnery Co., 1972), pp. 181–208.

4. Jon Elster, "Self-Realization in Work and Politics: The Marxist Conception of the Good Life," ed. Ellen Frankel Paul, et al., *Marxism and Liberalism* (Oxford: Basil Blackwell, 1986), pp. 96-126, esp. pp. 110–115.

5. This problem is admitted by many advocates of market socialism. See, e.g., Carol Gould, *Rethinking Democracy* (Cambridge: Cambridge University Press, 1983), pp. 254ff. on the need for "market regulatory commissions" to control abuses.

6. On the fallacy of "the more machinery, the better" see the discussion in Murray N. Rothbard, *Man, Economy, and State* (Princeton: D. Van Nostrand, 1962) vol. II, pp. 631–32.

7. Robert Nozick, "Who Would Choose Socialism?", *Reason* (May, 1978), pp. 22–23.

8. The first estimate is by Michael Ellman, *Socialist Planning* (Cambridge: Cambridge University Press, 1989), p. 106. The higher figure is in Mikhail Heller and Aleksandr M. Nekrich, *Utopia in Power* (New York: Summit Books, 1986), p. 242.

9. ibid., pp. 469–70.

10. Ellman, *Socialist Planning,* pp. 58–59.

11. David Schweickart, *Capitalism or Worker Control?*, pp. 168–70. Schweickart treats the difficulties cooperatives have in expanding as a problem for capitalism rather than for cooperatives.

12. David Miller, "Market Neutrality and the Failure of Cooperatives," *British Journal of Political Science,* vol. II (1981), pp. 302–29.

Index

153